In Between

CW00828686

A New Approach to Mediumship

Steven Cranston

First published in the UK in 2022.

The Soul Man Ltd
www.thesoulmanscotland.com

The moral right of Steven Cranston to be identified as the author of the work has been asserted by him in accordance with the Copyright, Designs and Patents Act 1988.

Edited by Regina Vereker

Cover design by Rebecca Hill
(Glowbug Design - glowbugdesign.com)

Back cover photography by Peter Lawson Photography

I dedicate this book to the Unseen World.

And to my wonderful Granny Helen Rodger who is now part of that Unseen World.

Steven Cranston also known as 'The Soul Man' (
most respected mediums. Steven owns and run
Soul Man and Friends in Broxburn, and this
welcoming space that people can come to r(
readings, Tarot readings and Mediumship readi
his very successful spiritual training academy
Academy, and welcomes hundreds of students e
understanding of the spiritual arts.

Steven has been a medium since birth, and has al
of the unseen world, he trained with the Spirituali
(SNU) and this training enabled him to put
awareness. However, Steven wanted more than \
and so began to seek his own understanding of t
and what his connection really meant - with the
aspect being kindness.

Across all of the training he delivers, kindness unde
he does enabling people to find their best self.
teaching meditation has also been a strong pas:
through the work of kindness he has helped people
He works with the public, charities, schools and ot
enabling them to tap into their own power through
kindness, and the practice of meditation and self-re(

Steven's mission is to regulate the spiritual inc
everyone is working from a place of kindness,
understanding with integrity and the ability to re(
people need more.

Steven was born in Edinburgh, Scotland and
Livingston, a small-town west of Edinburgh, with his
children.

Contents

A medium's job is to prove the existence of the human soul after physical death beyond reasonable doubt, and to look after themselves physically, mentally, and spiritually, so as they can be the best most conductive vessel for the spirit world.

"The Soul Man"

Chapter 1
The Whisperers

My whole childhood was about to be one full of little whispers from the spirit world.

I can hear the dull footsteps on the thick comforting carpets behind me as I lie in my bed and stare at the wall. It's the middle of the night and whoever this is has woken me from my sleep. I can feel their energy, it feels like a man, I hear his breath and my body freezes with fear. What if it is not one of the whisperers?

What if it is a real person who comes to kill children in their beds? I want to scream but I can't. I can hear the floorboards creaking as he approaches closer and closer. I can see my breath puffing like a cloud of smoke, and so I hold my breath hoping that he doesn't see the smoke signals, anything to stop him seeing me. I'm frozen in fear and don't know what to do. I know he's at my bedroom door now as I feel his glare on my back, and I instinctively know now that he doesn't want to hurt me, but I am still scared. My bedroom is a long rectangular shape. My bed is against the wall straight across from the door, my wardrobe sits at the end of my bed with my chest of drawers under the bedroom window, and a small bedside cabinet with my lamp on is the only light I have.

He's close now and my duvet is the only thing keeping me safe. At least, that's what I'm telling myself - nobody can get through a duvet right? I take deep breaths and try to calm down, but in these moments all I want to do is run to the safety of my Mum's bed. I'm frozen in fear. The air around me is still icy cold and I'm using what little movement I still have to plug the spaces in the duvet. He's right behind me. What does he want and why isn't he saying anything? I feel him looking at me again and it runs an icy cold feeling through my veins. My Mum and Dad are asleep in bed and my sister is asleep in her bed. It's late, perhaps 2 or 3 in the morning. They always come at this time. My fear begins to turn into something stronger, something more, it feels like anger or perhaps on reflection it is adrenaline, so with each passing second my strength builds and finally I pluck up the courage to prepare to turn around. My heart is beating faster and faster, the adrenaline is running through my veins, and the fear is replaced with a burst of energy as I spin around with tears filling my eyes and shout "MUM!"

He's gone. Gone without a trace. Mum appears moments later, and she fills the space he left with love. I tell her "there was a man here Mum, and he was scaring me. I couldn't move!" Mum looks around and calls out in an angry voice "leave him alone!" I am safe once again. She always knew what to say to make them go away. But where did he go and who was he? Why did he choose me? What did he want? He was a tall man, with a dark mysterious energy and would always appear at the top of the stairs, sometimes I could almost see his eyes. He was that menacing figure that haunted my safe space, and I could never pick up the courage to speak to him. Perhaps he wanted to give me a message, or perhaps he wanted to kill me in my sleep? What if he would never go away? I would later find out the startling evidence as to who this man was and what he wanted with me, but first I must tell you my story. My story of a caring, kind, and compassionate boy stuck in conflict between two worlds, never truly accepting either.

My name is Steven Cranston. I am also known as The Soul Man.

This is the story of my journey to being The Soul Man, a journey that started as a child with my awareness of souls around me. My story begins in Edinburgh, where I was the first of two children by my Mum and Dad. I have always had a very special relationship with my Mum and my Granny. I truly believe that the nurture I received from both my Mum and my Granny allowed me to be the most perfect canvas to work with for the spirit world. My earliest childhood memory of being aware of the spirit world is lying in my crib and feeling people around my crib whispering little whispers. As I heard these people whispering, I couldn't make out the words. I didn't know what they're saying but I knew that these people were not of this earth.

I was really lucky growing up, I had my Mum who showed us nothing but love. I felt secure and safe around her, which I feel gave me a firm foundation for coping with these little whispers around me. My Mum and Dad have both reported experiences that have creeped them out a little. Experiences like seeing their sensitive little child sitting in his highchair chatting away to invisible strangers. Recently I did an interview with my Mum on my online COVID lockdown show *The Soul Man Surgeries,* where she told me that as well as holding my hands out to invisible forces, I would babble away and speak to people who weren't there. This felt very normal to me, however, as I grew up I was always aware our house was so much fuller than just my family and myself, including my little sister.

My awareness of the spirit world came in many different stages across the years, my earliest memory is of what I call 'The Whisperers'. These visitors would be around me in the very early hours of the morning and at bedtime in the early evening. They were shadows that came with a low-pitched whispering of many voices - I could describe it like white noise or the whispers of 100 people. I would always feel them first before I saw them, this was usually accompanied by a change in temperature and my hairs standing on end. At times, the whispering was very overwhelming. On reflection, it was a lot for a child to experience. What is interesting is that even without them having a body I would feel their breath on my neck and hear their footsteps before I saw anything. You know the saying 'seeing is believing' well this is something that has never sat well with me because in my world feeling is believing. Sight is just one sense, but feeling is many more all rolled into one - touch, smell, hearing, knowing. I was aware of The Whisperers from a very young age until I was about 5 or 6 years old. Even at that young age, I somehow knew instinctively that they were my ancestors. People that looked and felt familiar - a lady with a purple hat on and piercing blue eyes; a small thin man around 5 feet tall with a flat cap on his head; a tall slim bald man; a man with a moustache and dark hair and his wife - they were all so loving towards me. They are my family from across the previous decades coming to celebrate my birth here on earth.

When I started school, things in my life changed quite significantly. On my first day at school, I remember feeling in the school, which was built in the 1950s/1960s, a very different energy than I had felt before. I was entering my educational years in many ways. On that first day, I remember sitting in the classroom and all of the parents were there standing behind each child, including my Mum standing proudly behind me. The parents went away but there were many other people left behind. On reflection, these people were not interacting with the other children, they were just observing. I remember clearly that these people did not dress normally, they appeared abstract and disconnected. There was an odd smell too, like the smell of an old wax jacket. They were with the parents looking down at us children, however only I was seeing The Whisperers. Despite knowing it was The Whisperers, I ignored them as I always did. Now I've seen some films where the departed don't leave people alone till they give a message, this wasn't my experience at all. Instead, they would look at me and smile. The way I see it is that they were visiting to watch milestone events just like the parents who had gone home. I no longer felt fear and this was probably the first time I could honestly say that I started understanding that they were not there to scare me, instead they were there as a support for us. To this day I still believe that these invisible beings, our ancestors, are with us every day inspiring us to be the best we can be, helping us on our human journey.

I felt like I was always the odd one out, always that strange friend that was aware of the emotions and feelings of others. I often questioned why I felt so much empathy for others, I'd feel a deep sense of sorrow for the people at school who kept quiet saying very little to other children. I wanted to spend time with them and be their friend, and more often than not they would become great friends to me. However, there was always that conflict within me to run with the crowd and be like my other friends. But was I being true to myself? The answer was no and even though I knew that the easier thing to do was to be like the others, I had to follow the feeling of being different. My friends never really understood my empathy, but they felt it massively as they always experienced kindness from me. Feeling empathy in such a strong way was a big part of who I was and am now. My concern for others' wellbeing has been an important part of my life, and I remember this occurrence at school very well. It wasn't just living people that were drawn to my empathy, it was spirit people too, but I wasn't aware of this until I was older.

I recall one particular time where I couldn't help but feel sorry for a boy in the playground who would play on his own. His name was Richard, and he would play at the wall in our playground with no one ever interacting with him. His clothes were scruffy, and he wore a blazer and a satchel school bag. Richard had a haunting silence about him, he was inherently sad, he always seemed a little odd and gave me a feeling he was much older than he appeared. Writing this I'm aware of the fact that I often feel people's energy first and this is no different with living people than it is with spirit people. It seemed to me that he always looked a little sad and always disappeared after break times. I never saw him inside of the school. He also played with marbles, another thing that was unusual to do at my school. I never once ever thought that Richard could be spirit, and for a long time I questioned whether he was spirit or a living boy. Many years later I came to the realisation that he wasn't alive, he was a spirit boy as no one else knew of him or spoke to him. What I do know is that I made his day better by just being around him. Years later, I had the opportunity to speak to the old playground supervisor, which confirmed my realisation that Richard was in fact spirit. She explained that I was always playing by the wall talking away to myself at break times. When I look back at this, I realise that this was the case, and I knew he was not of this world. He made me feel the same way spirit always has, my skin tingles, my senses become hyper focussed and time around me stops.

Death is a strange word to me, death means cease to exist, I've never experienced the end of anything, just a new beginning.

Steven Cranston

Chapter 2
Grandad

Over the years my connection with the spirit world changed many times, at each milestone of my life and by about the age of 9 I was no longer seeing the spirit world. But why? The reason is I hated it. I hated the fact that my friends all lived normal lives, but I had this exceptional other side of my life that none of them had. I was always really honest with my friends about what I saw and felt, they would laugh and say things like "I SEE DEAD PEOPLE" to me. It was just kids making fun of something they had no understanding of.

For a young lad experiencing an unseen world it's quite a traumatic thing to tell your most trusted friends and find that they do not understand it. Spending time with my friends who were normal lads who believed in what they could see and touch rather than what they could feel, they would often make fun of my empathy as it wasn't a normal thing for a lad our age. Girls are able to express warmth and feeling for each other without question but for boys it was seen as weakness in the early 1990s. However, I would never change who I was for anyone's opinion. I had a strong unshakeable belief of who I was and as long as I was kind that is all that mattered to me. It is virtually impossible for people to be unkind to someone who lives and breathes kindness. I would never understand the pecking order of the popular kids and the less popular kids at school, because I swiftly migrated between all groups within the playground, talking to the popular kids and the less popular kids, finding enriching experiences with each group. The common denominator between the groups was that they were all the same, just with different stories.

When I was 12, we moved to a bigger house, and this was when things really started changing again. We moved 10 miles away and we had the choice to move school or stay at our current school, but it would mean we would have to travel to school on the bus every day. Our new house was in the Sighthill area of Edinburgh, a maisonette with upstairs and downstairs, much bigger than our flat in Oxgangs. My Mum and I went to view the house before we moved in, we parked the car in the car park and walked up the two flights of stairs to a long landing with doors on the left. After four doors we came to an empty window with a large metal door, the local council had fitted the house with a burglar proof door. My Mum pulled the keys out of her bag with a brown tag attached to them saying 18/3, she fiddled the keys in the metal lock, and we walked into a large well-lit hallway. The moment we walked into the house, I felt an instant feeling of dread. My skin tingled, and the intense smell of leather and mould hit me. Remember my story at the start of the book, of the man who my Mum shooed away? This is the whole story. I started to feel dizzy and as I held onto the stair banister, I instantly saw a man lying at the foot of the stairs. I got such a fright, I looked at my Mum to tell her and it was clear she was feeling similar. "Someone has died in this house" she said to me. This confirmation from my Mum that I had seen the vision of the man led me to shock when my Mum agreed to take the house. So, we moved house, and Mum and Dad spent time decorating the house whilst we lived on pot noodles and chip shop dinners. It was such a great experience, but I couldn't help but feel that someone was watching, we were being observed by someone I couldn't see. After a few weeks of decorating, we all started to settle into our new home - my Mum, Dad, my sister and I, and our family dog Robbo. My bedroom was the box room which looked on to the top of the stairs, those same stairs where I had seen the man lying at the bottom. The space had a high ceiling and a long steep staircase, every time I stood at the top of the stairs, I would feel like I was going to be pushed down. Often, I would be lying in bed and feel my skin start to tingle and that musty smell would always come. At this point our dog Robbo would stand at the top of the stairs and growl at the air. Was he aware of someone that had not been around us until we moved into this house? I think to myself that the house is haunted. My Dad would say that perhaps he was just hearing the neighbours or passers-by, but I knew different, Robbo would stand guard against my invisible intruder every night.

Between 12am and 5am I could feel the energy in the house change. I woke in the early hours one morning, skin tingling and fear gripping me, something wasn't right. The house felt cold and empty, and I found the courage to look at the top of the stairs. I was frozen in fear as a man's shape stood looking back at me. "Who are you?" I said, I could feel his head turn towards me and the house would start to warm gently as he faded away without saying anything. Then at other times I would see him and get some interaction with him. This went on for months and over time I began to accept his presence as someone who didn't want to hurt us. I always wondered about what had happened to him, why was he lying at the bottom of our stairs? We later found out that our house had in fact been the scene of a crime in which a man was hit across the head and fell downstairs, his body was found at the bottom of the stairs just like I had seen.

My Grandad was my Mum's Dad, he separated from my Granny when my Mum was young, so I actually had the privilege of having two Grandads on my Mum's side. Grandad, my Mum's dad, was such an amazing man. So kind, so gentle, and always had us out walking. He was a gardener and so it was really important for him to be outdoors. He was 5ft with white hair that stood on end in every direction, he had a big nose and the warmest blue eyes. He had one leg shorter than the other and had a high-pitched voice with a wee whistle at the end of his words. He loved to walk, sing, and play football with the local kids just outside his house. I spoke to my Grandad about my experiences with the spirit world, which he always found really fascinating and would ask me lots of questions about who I had seen this week. One time, we were waiting on the bus to go into town in the evening and I could see this unusual bus coming towards us, it was an older looking bus with a large indent on the passenger side and I said to my Grandad "here's the bus", he looked at me and said, "what bus?". When I turned back around, the bus was gone. There was no explanation for this, but I had seen the number on the bus and as I explained to my Grandad what the number of the bus was, he said, "that bus hasn't been on this route for years, maybe it was a ghost bus!" and he laughed.

One Sunday, after staying with Grandad, I was in bed and had this feeling of dread that my Grandad didn't have long to live. He had an ulcer in his stomach but other than that he was in good health. My Mum said "Steven, Grandad's okay, stop worrying", so I put this down to my sensitivity and the fear of losing the people I loved. I was 12 years old, almost 13. I was aware over the coming weeks something wasn't right, I couldn't put my finger on it, I just knew that something felt off, it felt strange and wrong. To let you know the type of person my Grandad was, he really was very funny, he would let us cover him in make-up, paint his toenails and give us full permission to cook up the strangest concoctions in his kitchen. He would take us swimming every Friday night to the Commonwealth swimming pool in Edinburgh where I learned to swim on my own. My Grandad, however, could never swim, and he would bob along in the shallow end of the pool whilst we swam around like dolphins. One time, he was pretending he was drowning. We laughed thinking it was hilarious before we then realised that he was in deeper water, and he actually was almost drowning! The lifeguard had to jump into the pool and save him, something that we would laugh about even to this day. Afterwards, we would then go down to a local cafeteria called Brattisani, and if you live in Edinburgh and remember it, you will know that they did the most amazing knickerbocker glory, which was the highlight of the whole trip every Friday evening. I loved the theatre of the large glass filled with ice cream and fresh strawberries, this made me feel so much love. He didn't have much, but this £2.50 sundae was his way of showing us how much he loved us. I believe that anybody who knew my Grandad felt a massive positive change in their life as a result of their connection to him.

In November that year, about 8 weeks after my initial feeling of dread, things changed forever. I was about to experience my first ever loss. My feelings were right about Grandad, something wasn't right. My sister and I were going to Grandad's for our usual weekend stint. It was a Thursday, and Mum and Dad were both working, so we were staying over at Grandad's and going to school from there the next day. We hopped on the number 52 bus at about 7pm and we got there around 7.30pm. Walking down towards his house from the bus stop it was dark as it was the end of November, and we were desperate to get into his house to get warmed up. When we arrived, something didn't feel right. I had this feeling in the pit of my stomach, I don't know what it was, but I just knew something wasn't right. The flat was in darkness as we approached. Grandad lived in the bottom flat of the high-rise flats in Gracemount, Edinburgh. He had a balcony that led straight onto the street with his own gate that gave access into his lounge. The house that was always illuminated with warm light shining through the net curtains was now in darkness. This was a very strange sight for us, and as we approached, the feeling of dread increased. I knew that Grandad wasn't there. We knocked on the balcony door which was the usual entry point. There was no answer, so we walked round to the front door again but still no answer. At a loss for what to do to get into the flat, my sister borrowed a screwdriver from a neighbour and we somehow managed to get the front door open.

When we walked in, the house was in darkness, it was still and cold. At the front door, the electricity box sat to the left and we could not get the power to come on. We walked up the long hallway and tried to get into the living room but there was a chair against the living room door. Now, my Grandad always did this before he went to bed, he would push a chair against the door and he never slept in a bed, he always slept on the sofa in the living room. When we eventually got into the living room after pushing the door away, we saw Grandad lying on the sofa. He was so still, so very still. In this moment, all time stood still, everything was silent. I now believe that the electricity not coming on was my Grandad's doing because if there was a well-lit room, I believe what we were about to realise would have been much worse. We walked into that room and the one thing I remember was the stillness and the cold. I could see Grandad lying on the couch so quiet, so still. The streetlights outside shone through the net curtains illuminating his pale skin and bright white hair. We approached him and my sister touched the back of his leg which felt like cold marble, she ran out the house screaming to get help.

Was he dead? The man I idolised couldn't possibly be dead? He wasn't ill and had been fine the week before. At that moment, when my sister had run out, I felt a sudden urge to sit with him. As I sat with my Grandad's cold hard body not fully realising the magnitude of what was happening, I then heard a familiar voice, my Grandad's voice. I could hear him behind me, as clear as I hear someone's voice right now. He said "Steven, I have died. I need you to phone 999, get an ambulance, then phone your Dad and tell him to come and collect you and your sister". Instantly I could feel all that love, all that joy, all that happiness, everything that made him behind me, and I felt his gentle hands on both of my shoulders. I knew at that moment that he had died because what I could see in front of me was not what I could feel behind me. I calmly picked up the phone dialled 999 and said to the operator "you need to send an ambulance. My Grandad has died." The call handler then asked me how I knew my Grandad had died and I replied, "because he has told me he has died". I gave her the address and hung up the phone. When I picked the phone back up, I then called my Dad and told him what had happened. I put a blanket over my Grandad or what was left of him, his body, and held his hand until the paramedics came. They came in with torches and said, "we need you to leave him now son, we will help him from here." After that I found myself in the next-door neighbour's house sitting on the sofa waiting for my Dad to arrive, my Mum was working, and he had to call her at work to tell her what had happened from the neighbour's house. I will never forget hearing my Mum screaming on the phone that day. In the last year or so of my Grandad's life there was much heartache, he lost his dogs, Ally and Pepi, which absolutely devastated him, but he kept smiling and always doing so much for others. I like to think of myself as a younger version of him.

My Grandad's death triggered something in me and on reflection it may have been happening alongside puberty, I was 13 and so I was going through lots of changes. My voice was getting deeper, I was growing, my soul was changing, my understanding of the spirit world was deepening. I started to experience the world very differently. For my whole life I had been the observer with the spirit world but now I knew I could be much more than just an observer. I have always been able to connect with the souls of people who were no longer in this physical world. So, I decided to ask for proof. I said out loud "Grandad, please come and visit me." Two weeks after he passed, I was lying in my bed sleeping that night and, again in those hours between midnight and 5am, I woke up to see my Grandad standing by the side of my bed. He had light all around him and I'd love to tell you the exciting story that he had an aura of light, but I'm sorry to tell you that was actually the hall light shining behind him! He stood there and I asked him strangely "Grandad, has heaven rejected you or something?" He replied, "No son, I can come and see you whenever you want me to, all you need to do is ask." He then asked me for a hug, so I hugged him, and he felt as real as my hand feels on my arm right now. I could even feel the corrugated pattern in his jumper. From that day I have always known that my Grandad walks close to me, I can feel his influence, and although he's not there all the time, I know he's always got an eye on me guiding me and helping me when I need him.

Interestingly, my Mum also had a visit from my Grandad that evening. My Mum had got up to use the bathroom in the middle of the night and looked into my room to check on me. As she looked, she thought she saw someone but dismissed it as just the posters on my wall. When I woke up in the morning, I came downstairs, got my breakfast, and sat in the living room with my Mum and Dad. My Mum looked at me and said "Steven, what did you dream about last night?" I looked at her a little confusedly and said "Mum, I had a visit from Grandad. It felt very real, and I know that it was more than just a dream. Grandad came to visit me and I hugged him. He then walked out of my room and walked into your room." My Dad looked at my Mum and his jaw dropped. Before I had entered the room, my Mum had just told him how she was in bed and she heard my Grandad talking to her. He called her by the nickname he used for her, Sissy. He said that he had been to see me and had now come to see her, however, she wasn't able to see him, she could only hear his voice. Over the years, we've always felt my Grandad's influence around us. We've always been able to tell when he comes into the room, we've been able to smell him and just get a sense that he is there.

A grandfather is someone with silver in his hair and gold in his heart.

Author unknown

Finding the Medium Within You - 1

These subchapters are designed to help you find the fascinating truth of the medium within you. You are a soul with a body, therefore you have the ability to sense the unseen world. I've added mini exercises in some of these sections and I'd encourage you to take a notebook or write your notes in the back if the book in the section notes at the end......

I hope you enjoy

All my love

Steven x

Have you ever been sitting and randomly smelled your granny's perfume or felt her words in your head? I'm sure you have but if you haven't then you can train yourself to do this! How can I train myself to sense the spirit world I hear you ask? My friend it's simple. You are a spirit person in a physical body! So of course, you can develop your senses to a point in which you can tap into that space between your thoughts - your superconscious. Take some time to think about your experiences in life so far and I'm sure you will be able to remember a time when you have sensed something from the spirit world. In this chapter I've spoken about the tingling feeling and the smells I experience. These are my senses hyper focused and bypassing the rational conscious mind, filtering down through the subconscious and into the superconscious where my mind makes sense of it, and in return it is experienced by all three states in a wonderful collaborative way through my whole being. That is why people report these experiences as very emotional and mediums often describe their work as draining, but there is a way you can avoid feeling drained that I will talk about later.

If you have ever sensed a loved one who has passed, then you will likely look for reasoning for what you experienced and try to make sense of it. A good friend of mine refers to this as a higher power moment, and when we experience these things, often we tend to put it down as a dream or something other than supernatural. Our dreams are our minds' way of making sense of our days, helping our subconscious mind to make sense of the experiences the conscious mind has during the day. But are you aware of the superconscious mind? Take the subconscious mind, it can only be activated as a result of the experiences the conscious mind has. However, the superconscious is activated through the subconscious which has a less rational understanding of our reality. This is why we experience our loved ones in our dreams because the conscious mind is asleep so the subconscious and superconscious simply accept the augmented reality.

The subconscious mind processes information as an automatic response, so when we experience things through our conscious five senses, the subconscious mind automatically filters the information. When we tap into the superconscious, it makes sense of the experiences of both (often known as the ether, universe, or the space between our thoughts). The superconscious is where we experience deep spiritual experiences, have a knowing that we are on the right path, express creativity or tap into the universe for inspiration. Our five senses (sight, taste, touch, smell, and hearing) are all filtered through the conscious mind, but when developing mediumship, you can tap into the clair senses. I'll explain more about the clair senses later on, but essentially the clair senses are extensions of the physical senses that speak directly to your subconscious (your automatic knowing) that leads directly to the superconscious, and it is in those spaces between your own thoughts that we can tap into the energy of our passed loved ones.

My whole life I've been called a dreamer, and now I finally understand. The dreamer is the alchemist of the spiritual realms, able to understand this superconscious reality because they have always been tapped into. My whole childhood, every time I have sensed the spirit world, all of my senses are activated. Animals do this all the time, their very acute senses take over and they trust that something invisible is there that they can't see. To think that it only exists if we can see it is a little narrow minded considering all of our other senses are activated. The rational conscious mind doesn't understand it so the subconscious and the superconscious have taken over and shown it in a way my conscious mind can understand.

Is this the spirit world, Angels, or psychic ability? I will tell you exactly what it is and how to connect with your own loved ones in the simplest way, it is so simple and is the best way to connect. I call it - being your own medium.

Take some notes: Have you ever sensed the spirit world with your other senses? What did this experience mean to you?

The true sign of intelligence is not knowledge BUT imagination.

Albert Einstein

Chapter 3
Coming of Age

So, at this point I am now 14 or 15 years old and well into the swing of puberty, my voice is deepening, and I am becoming a man. My awareness of my own self is changing along with my awareness of the spirit world. I believe that the different stages of life dictate the way in which we perceive energy. For instance, I feel things very differently now as opposed to when I was a young lad. I have more empathy and even more understanding of the man I am, which blends amazingly well with my mediumship.

By the age of 15, I was 6ft tall and had really come into my own spiritual awareness. At this point I was more acutely aware of the subtle changes around me and also the change in energy with people living. I needed help, but who could help me? Who could understand? So, I asked the spirit world, "if you want me, you need to show me a good teacher". After so much stress of losing my Grandad and finding his body, it was hard to keep on top of my emotions. I was a teenage boy who had lost someone incredibly important to me, and then had a profound spiritual experience at the same time. This was the first time that I had proof and contact from my own loved one, evidence that was relatable and not just being aware of people around me. My Grandad had orchestrated the events of that night so that I would be okay and able to cope with what was a highly stressful situation. I went back to school after a few weeks off and my friends were aware of what had happened, but I wasn't coping. I wanted my Grandad to be around me all the time and he wasn't. I missed him so much and just wanted to tell him how much I loved him. I couldn't get him out of my head and I just wanted to live in the space between my thoughts, the superconscious, but I couldn't because my conscious mind had so much to process. I was thinking and not feeling. Any feelings I had were grief, that painful gut-wrenching hollow ache that moves from the middle of your chest and consumes your entire body. The emotional pain was unbearable, and I could feel myself thinking irrationally. For the first time ever, I was feeling the emotions of anger and envy. Why did other people still have their grandad? My Grandad was special, why would God take such a good person? I became angry with the spirit world too, often screaming into the air, feeling deeply that they took him away from me.

French class was my third lesson of the day, and the teacher wasn't familiar to me. She was a stand in, one of the guidance teachers in fact. She started her lesson, but I wasn't listening, I was somewhere else thinking about that night of finding my Grandad's body but feeling him behind me, talking to me. She was a small lady, with dark brown hair, and known for her very strict nature, she scared me a little if I'm very honest. Suddenly I was aware of the class sniggering around me and the teacher standing over me snapping a wooden ruler into the palm of her hand. "Mr Cranston, are you with us?" she said. Her whole demeanour was intimidating, and I felt completely embarrassed that she had taken the opportunity to humiliate me when I was in so much pain. I didn't respond but I could feel this awful dark energy moving up through my chest which I can only describe as hatred and anger in liquid form. "MR CRANSTON" she shouted. The ringing in my ears activated the volcanic eruption within me. I blew up screaming at her "LEAVE ME ALONE", the anger then instantly overflowed and turned to emotion in the form of tears. I couldn't stop crying, the emotion was choking me and my heart was breaking in two. I've never felt so much pain and sorrow in one go. It was very clear at this point that she was very aware that she had acted badly, and she dismissed the whole class and made a call. I sat in a daze completely numb until she gently touched my shoulder saying "Steven, I'm very sorry I upset you." In that second the kindness she showed me completely diffused the pain and all that rage was replaced with more tears but tears of sadness and empathy for her, as well as me. "It's okay, my

Grandad died, and I miss him so much". She rubbed my shoulder again and said, "oh darling, come with me, let's get you a cup of tea and a biscuit." This was the first and only time I ever had a cup of tea at school. The guidance base was basically a big office where the teachers would sit. All of the teachers that day showed me so much kindness as I spilled my story on how I had found my Grandad dead in the weeks before.

After that conversation took place, I was referred to see a professional at the Royal Edinburgh Hospital by the school's guidance counsellor and relevant professional body. I needed help to deal with the emotional aspect of things, but I was about to receive much more than I expected. My appointment was just as I left school. I had just turned 16 years old a few days before. It felt strange attending as I felt that so much time had passed by since my Grandad's death. The main part of the hospital was familiar. I had walked past it many times before, but although the corridors were well lit, it felt overwhelming. I didn't know where I was going, so I asked a few people who got me to the right place. I thought I was going to see a counsellor. The receptionist said, "your appointment is with the mental health team" which made me a little worried as I thought "oh no they don't think I'm nuts do they?" I sat in a small waiting room with blue plastic high backed chairs staring at the children's toys in the corner by the magazines. "Steven Cranston" a short lady with ginger hair called, peeping her head round the door frame. The room resembled a doctor's room with a bed in the corner and all the usual apparatus a doctor has. There were two nurses in the room, and I was asked if the second nurse could stay to observe. I agreed and she told me she was going to ask me a lot of questions and I had to answer honestly and also that there was no judgement, and certainly no right or wrong answers. She asked me many questions about my life, my childhood, my relationship with my parents and then about my connection with spirit. I remember one of those questions was "do you hear voices?" and "do you see people others can't see?" I knew from all my experiences with friends and family previously that this meant they didn't believe me and maybe thought I was going nuts, so I told them "listen I know that on your form you will think that I'm nuts, but I need to tell you that I'm not. I have always felt them around me. I am not unwell, I feel really mentally well. I'm about to go to college and everything I've ever seen, nobody believes. I'm okay with that but I'm not unwell." The nurse replied, "we know you aren't unwell Steven, that's really clear to us, but we want to understand what's going on so we can help you better. Well, do you see anyone around me?" So, I focussed on her and I could feel a man blend around her left side. He was around 5ft 5 inches, short grey hair, with a kind smile. When he looked at me, I just knew he had passed with a heart defect, not a heart attack but his heart just stopped. When I told her this, the nurse got visibly upset and her eyes filled with tears. She then left the room for a few moments to compose herself and when she came back in, she thanked me and told me that what I had said had given her great comfort.

When I arrived at my appointment that day, I had no idea that the nurses at the hospital would guide me on my path to the place that would become my spiritual home. The help and kindness that the nurses showed me that day is something I will never forget. They suggested to me that it would be possibly helpful for me to go see a spiritualist as they may be able to help me with that side of things. A spiritualist? What was a spiritualist? It must have something to do with speaking to the dead, surely? I sat on the bus on the way home racking my brain as to what it could be, maybe someone who tells my fortune like Whoopie Goldberg in the film Ghost? This was a film that resonated highly with me at certain parts, except for floating pennies and shadow creatures dragging bad people away after death! But I had never heard of the word spiritualist before. So, when I got home that day, I checked the Yellow Pages for Spiritualists (we didn't have Google then) and the first listing was Edinburgh Spiritualist Society, 34 Albany Street.

At first, I didn't do anything about it for a while, unsure what to do or how to process what they had said. However, as it happens, spirit always has a way to nudge me in the right direction. Sometime later I asked my cousin if she would like to go out one night to get out of the house and she said she couldn't as she had a reading at the local spiritualist church in Albany Street, Edinburgh. It seemed like divine intervention to me, I was finally given the opportunity to visit the church and so I went with her. Not knowing what to expect, I found myself alone while my cousin was upstairs in the church getting her reading. There was a blue door which opened on one side of a much larger door, which itself opened into a small porch area with a wooden bench on the left and to the right, a glass case and visitor book. The floor was covered in wobbly mosaic tiles leading through a glass door into a grand hallway with a staircase to the right and three doors with ornate cornice surrounding the door frames. The President of Edinburgh Spiritualist Church happened to be the first face I saw when I walked through the doors of Albany Street. She looked at me and asked what I was doing here. I replied, "I don't know how I'm here, but I'm here." She looked at me and said, "You're obviously meant to be here." I was invited to stay after my cousin had her reading to the open awareness circle. The room it was held in was the first room on the left after the wobbly mosaic tiled floor. The room had silver and gold wallpaper, a beautiful fireplace, a piano to the right, and a large circle of chairs around a smaller table with a candle in the centre. Your eyes were naturally drawn up to the elaborate gold cornice ceiling that looked like something from a Greek temple.

The president switched off the lights and instructed us to close our eyes and see what we could perceive for 10 minutes. As I closed my eyes soft melodic music played in the background and a familiar scent filled the room, old leather and mould. My skin fizzed with electricity tingling from my head to my toes, much more intense than I had ever felt it before. Perhaps this place was like a tv aerial, boosting my signal. Soon I felt the room filling with spirit people, all eager to speak to the other people sitting in the room. It was almost like this room was a conduit for the spirit world. During this open awareness circle, I saw a beautiful lady dancing in the middle of the room with a bright yellow dress. She made eye contact with me and said "hello, my name is Elaine and that is my husband, Jim." She pointed to one of the men sitting in the circle with me. Also, during this experience, I saw lots of images, lots of things moving through my mind. The gaps within my own thoughts became consumed with images like Egyptian hieroglyphics, numbers, and swirls of colour. Time felt as though it stopped, and I was so surprised it had only been 10 minutes. After the time was up, everyone in the circle was asked to share with the rest of the group what they had seen and what they had perceived. When it was my turn, I told them of my experience where I was aware of a lady whose name was Elaine and that she pointed to the gentleman sitting across from me. I told them that was her husband. The man, Jim, got quite emotional, and the president said to me "yes son he can take all of that information, well done." Afterwards, Jim came across to me and shook my hand. He said "son, I have waited years to hear that message. Elaine was my wife and I miss her so much."

Over the years I attended Albany Street I created a really good friendship with Jim. He was then in his 70s and is now in the spirit world. So many people that I knew back in those days are now part of the spirit world. Mediums, healers, and people who attended services every week. It makes me sad that they are no longer here but again, I am so comforted in their knowledge and their belief of the spirit world. I am comforted that they are exactly where they need to be now. I was finally home. I was finally in a place where other people understood me, around other people who had the same experiences as me. Other people knew what it was like to grow up feeling this way. For the first time in my life, I felt a sense of belonging, I could speak to these people without judgement as they could relate and had had similar experiences to my own. Albany Street Spiritualist Church was run by the governing body of Spiritualists in the UK, the Spiritualists' National Union (SNU), and being hungry for knowledge and understanding of my gift I wanted to know more. It was important that I understood everything there was to know about my role as a medium, so I undertook training on my own with the support of the society in Albany Street, calling it home or my base. Every Thursday there was an evening of clairvoyance where mediums from all over the UK would visit and give evidence of the spirit world to a congregation of up to 50 people in the platform room upstairs. The platform room was a long Lshaped room, and at the top corner there was a platform built-in to the left side of the room. On this platform there were three or four chairs and a large throne looking chair that would be taken usually by the President of Albany Street. There were large purple curtains that covered the 10-foot windows and an old wooden lectern that overlooked a piano that sat just below the platform in front. We would sing spiritualist hymns with the hymn books provided.

My favourite hymn was always 'Open my eyes.' The reason being was because I felt it helped me to open up to the energy of the spirit world by opening up my senses.

"Open my eyes, that I may see

Glimpses of truth thou hast for me;

Place in my hands the wonderful key

That shall unclasp and set me free

Silently now I wait for thee

Ready, my God, thy will to see

Open my eyes, illumine me, Spirit divine!

Open my ears, that I may hear

Voices of truth thou sendest clear;

And while the wavenotes fall on my ear

Everything false will disappear

Silently now I wait for thee

Ready, my God, thy will to see

Open my ears, illumine me, Spirit divine!

Open my mouth, and let me bear

Gladly the warm truth everywhere;

Open my heart and let me prepare

Love with thy children thus to share

Silently now I wait for thee

Ready, my God, thy will to see
Open my heart, illumine me, Spirit divine!

On a Sunday, the Divine service would take place from 6:30pm with a public address added in. I watched in awe one evening as a wonderful medium spoke about the dragonfly story. This wonderful analogy really made me think long and hard about my Grandad and the spirit world that has surrounded me throughout my life. This is the story…

Down below the surface of a quiet pond lived a little colony of water bugs. They were a happy colony, living far away from the sun. For many months they were very busy, scurrying over the soft mud on the bottom of the pond. They did notice that every once in a while, one of their colony seemed to lose interest in going about the mud and started to climb the stem of a pond lily. Clinging to the stem of a pond lily, it gradually moved out of sight and was seen no more.
"Look!" said one of the water bugs to another. "One of our colony is climbing up the lily stalk. Where do you think she is going?" Up – up – up it slowly went…. even as they watched, the water bug disappeared from sight. Its friends waited and waited but it didn't return…
"That's funny!" said one water bug to another. "Wasn't she happy here?" asked a second… "Where do you suppose she went?" wondered a third.
No one had an answer. They were greatly puzzled. Finally, one of the water bugs, a leader in the colony, gathered its friends together. "I have an idea. The next one of us who climbs up the lily stalk must promise to come back and tell us where he or she went and why."
"We promise" – they replied solemnly.
One spring day, not long after, the very water bug who had suggested the plan found himself climbing up the lily stalk. Up, up, up, he went. Before he knew what was happening, he had broken

through the surface of the water and fallen onto the broad, green lily pad above.

When he awoke, he looked about with surprise. He couldn't believe what he saw. A startling change had come to his old body. His movement revealed four silver wings and a long tail. Even as he struggled, he felt an impulse to move his wings...The warmth of the sun soon dried the moisture from the new body. He moved his wings again and suddenly found himself up above the water. He had become a dragonfly!!

Swooping and dipping in great curves, he flew through the air. He felt exhilarated in the new atmosphere. By and by, the new dragonfly lighted happily on a lily pad to rest. Then it was that he chanced to look below to the bottom of the pond. Why, he was right above his old friends, the water bugs! There they were scurrying around, just as he had been doing some time before. The dragonfly remembered the promise: the next one of us who climbs up the lily stalk will come back and tell where he or she went and why. Without thinking, the dragonfly darted down. Suddenly he hit the surface of the water and bounced away. Now that he was a dragonfly, he could no longer go into the water...

"I can't return!" he said in dismay. "At least, I tried. But I can't keep my promise. Even if I could go back, not one of the water bugs would know me in my new body. I guess I'll just have to wait until they become dragonflies too. Then they'll understand what has happened to me, and where I went."

The Dragonfly is a symbol of transition and change and is so important to me that I chose it as the main body of the logo we use for what was yet to become my wonderful business, The Soul Man and Friends.

Over the years I watched other mediums work, and I picked up techniques and better ways of working. I always sat at the back of the room to give the working mediums my respect and energy. I worked through my workbooks, understanding the philosophy of mediumship, as well as speaking and demonstrating with the correct decorum. I would have a small workbook that would be signed by the president or booking secretary of the churches I visited. Visiting churches was something that took so much time, I was always booked for churches and before long I was out five evenings a week - spiritualism had taken over all of my free time and I felt part of this massive loving extended family. By this point I was 20 years old, and I had clocked up 960 hours of platform work and given around 1200 messages across the public platform. Visiting all over Scotland and England and making many friends over the years with other mediums who did the same as me, I began to know so many people. Often when I was visiting churches and centres, I would recognise the names of the mediums who would be on the week after me. I have always been very grateful for the chance to help heal the two worlds. Before long I would notice the same people in the congregation attending different churches and centres miles apart. People seemed to love my honest approach to my work and my hard-working ethic and wanted to see me more often.

True belonging only happens when we present our authentic, imperfect selves to the world, our sense of belonging can never be greater than our level of self-acceptance

Brene Brown

Finding the Medium Within You – 2

Now an adult and in the full swing of my mediumship, I was able to relate to other adults who would stop me after services to say they had spiritual experiences that they couldn't explain.

Have you had a spiritual experience as an adult that you couldn't explain? And how does it feel? As an adult, we try to make sense of things, usually putting it down to wishful thinking or coincidence. Usually as an adult people want to develop that sense, or completely shut it out. The most common thing people experience is a feeling like someone is in their house, usually thinking it's haunted. Or after a big event in life people often see things differently and start feeling and experiencing their passed loved ones through dreams, or in their waking life with no explanation as to why. My first port of call is always to ask someone to rationalise things and if they feel unwell or are showing signs of poor emotional health to see their GP first. However, if like me, you are presenting to be mentally well and have a good support network, then chances are you are experiencing the gaps between your subconscious and superconscious. You are getting snippets between your own thoughts of the spirit world. With time and patience, you can train these gaps to get bigger giving you better focus on the superconscious. Is this the spirit world, Angels, or psychic ability? The truth is these gaps are a combination of all of the above. With time and skill, you can start to separate them and understand what is you, what is the spirit world and what is more than that, Angels.

I'd like to show you how to connect with your own loved ones in the spirit world. But first let's discuss feeling drained, why do people feel drained when they work as mediums? A medium's job is to prove the existence of the human soul beyond reasonable doubt and look after themselves spiritually, physically, and emotionally so they can be the best channel to the superconscious. A medium up there on a platform or sitting with you telling you what is happening in your life and telling you about the dream man or woman that's about to enter your life, is going to feel drained. Nobody can ever tell you what is going to happen in your life because you have free will. If that is the goal of their work to impress you by fortune telling then that is for their own self-gratification, which is exhausting, and they will eventually be caught out or burn out. They are simply using so much of their energy to connect, they are pushing and reaching to make a connection. Have you ever done a cryptic crossword or anything that takes lots of mind power to get the answers you need? It's draining, isn't it? That's what happens to a medium who doesn't give the energy over to the superconscious. When I work with the spirit world, I hand over and put my full trust in them. I let the words flow to me easily and I respond. I trust the emotions and the feelings in my body. I trust the words I feel and hear. I trust the smells I experience. I relay the information with kindness and respect to the recipient and it is received with so much gratitude by the recipient, it's like giving someone flowers! You make them feel good, so you get the buzz from doing something to make someone feel good. However, if you are giving flowers only to make you feel good then you are trying too hard to do something that is unnatural. It will feel difficult and take all of your energy because you are not doing it for the right reason, you are doing it for self-gratification. It is the same with the spirit world, if you are so caught up on being right then you aren't working authentically, you are only working for your own self-gratification and not that of the spirit world. So of course, the medium who does these things will feel frazzled because it is all about them, and not the sitter.

I see myself as the wonderful messenger who is able to pass over healing and love beyond reasonable doubt by trusting the gentle messages that sit between my thoughts in the superconscious. I would like to teach you a 10-minute technique to help you tap into the wonderful gift that is being your own medium.

First of all, you need to sit relaxed and comfortable and the best way to do this is sitting up (to stop you falling asleep)! It is important you relax your body fully first, so I suggest doing a ten-minute body scan meditation as this is a great way of doing this. We offer a body scan meditation on our YouTube channel - The Soul Man and Friends TV. Once you have fully relaxed your body, then you are in a more receptive place for this technique.

The meditation I will take you through now can also be found on our YouTube channel named 'Connecting with the spirit world':

Imagine yourself in a space with no windows or doors. A relaxing space that feels warm and safe. Feel this space expand and imagine a warm white light in the distance within this space, then slowly imagine a crowd of people moving out from this light towards you. As you imagine it becomes your reality as you access the superconscious through your subconscious dream-like state.

You begin to see familiar shapes, the shapes of the people you love who have passed to the spirit world, remember their smell, their touch, the way they made you feel in their company and spend time in this wonderful meeting space with them. When the time is right and you have the time with them that you wanted to, then simply see them walk back into the light and the light fades.

Then open your eyes and revel in the wonder that even just for a small moment you have connected with their love again, the more you do it the stronger it gets, and different people step forward each time. If it is someone specific, you want then simply intend it.

- **What did your experience mean to you?**
- **How did you feel afterwards?**

Take some notes of your experience and repeat it as often as you like.

This is a simple but incredibly powerful way for you to be your own medium. It takes practice, and patience, however, you have the ability to be your own medium, and this meditation allows you to connect with your loved ones.

Developing as a medium takes time. It needs you to be able to feel more than you possibly have done before, and a fundamental lesson in perfecting your mediumship is kindness. I'll speak more in the next section about this, and how crucial it is as a medium. Yes, folks you read that right, kindness is the greatest lesson in being a medium. It will transform the way you work.

Meditation can help us embrace our worries, our fear, our anger; and that is very healing. We let our own natural capacity of healing do the work.

Thich Nhat Hanh

Chapter 4
True Love

I was so busy working full time with the spirit world, I needed a more flexible job that made my spiritual work easier to manage. I was a trained pastry chef, and the split shifts and long hours were just not working for me. I managed to get a job at the local bingo hall in Fountainbridge, Edinburgh, which I would later discover was the old Palais de Danse that Jim and his wife danced in! My role here was to let the cleaning team in, change light bulbs and do basic maintenance work, a really easy job, but could be really boring. The cleaners were my main source of interaction. "We have a new girl starting today" said the cleaning supervisor, "She's my friend's daughter." I remember replying "Ahh cool, look forward to meeting her" as I stood at the door at 8am. Before long, white trainers, tight jeans and a denim jacket came into my view, a girl with her hair scraped back in a tight ponytail started tapping on the glass. I'm thinking *wow this can't be the cleaner!* I open the door and say "Hi, can I help you?" This beautiful girl replies "Yeah I'm Nicola, this is my first shift."

I had heard of love at first sight but didn't ever believe it would happen to me. I was smitten, I couldn't stop looking at her, *'she's way out of my league'* I thought to myself. I was fascinated by her and wanted to know more about her, and so after a few mornings sitting with the cleaning team I soon found out more about who she was. It was there that I discovered that she had two children. Knowing myself and what I was capable of, I kept thinking that I couldn't be a stepdad at my then age of 20. So, despite being so amazed by her, I tried to pull myself back. However, life does not always work the way you think it will. I could not help wanting to speak with Nicky, I was pulled towards her and found her so interesting. The other cleaning girls would say "Steven's a medium!" and much to my relief Nicky had been told before she started that there was a guy who worked there that was a medium, so she expected it and was okay with it. Although I was not able to make the jump into being a stepdad, I kept wanting to connect with her beautiful energy and make her see me as something more than just someone she worked with. I spent a lot of time talking to her and trying to make her laugh. One time, I joked with her "When we are married, I'll be out working 5 nights a week mind!" To my delight she replied, "Yeah, I'm okay with that, who knew what I'd be getting into marrying a medium!". At the time it was funny, and we laughed, but little did we know our love would fully blossom into something truly wonderful.

A few months passed and to my dismay Nicky decided it was time to leave the job as she could not get childcare. I felt worried, I realised that I wanted this girl in my life, whether I was ready for kids at 20 years old or not. I would learn to be ready. She was wonderful and I couldn't imagine not seeing her again, but how would we stay in touch? We weren't in a relationship and haven't even kissed! Nicky took the lead and gave me her number. Having exchanged phone numbers, it was not as simple as typing them into a mobile phone, back then mobile phones were not used too much. As it happened, Nicky phoned me first from a phone box asking how I was. Hearing her voice at the end of the line was amazing. I was so happy to speak to her and was desperate to see her, so we arranged to meet, and we drove to Hillend ski slope to look out across Edinburgh. Seeing Nicky outside of work and being with her alone was so special. This amazing girl had agreed to see me and on the special first date, we shared our first kiss. It was electric. My lips tingled and butterflies filled my body. I had never felt anything like it. Just being in her company made me feel like something I hadn't felt before, and I wondered if she felt it too. We sat for a while conscious that we didn't have long before I had to drop her off, and I knew I couldn't live without her. However, things progressed quickly between us, and after some time we decided to move in together. It was then that we moved to a new area, West Lothian, a new start for us.

Nicky and I were so in love, and I knew that for me the next important thing to do was make our devotion to each other official, so I asked her dad if I could marry Nicky. He said yes and I went shopping for a ring. On Valentine's Day 2004 I carefully blindfolded Nicky, sat her in the car and we drove to Hillend. I had a small bottle of champagne that I had hid under her seat and I drove with anticipation, my heart beating out of my chest. What if she said no? What would I do? What would that mean? I guess I'll find out soon! What surprised me most is that during this time building this wonderful new love with Nicky, my work with the spirit world was getting stronger and stronger, my connection was feeling very sharp and now on reflection it was because I truly was loving myself. I was happy on every level, I now had two amazing kids that I had easily learned to love as my own, and this amazing woman who thought the world of me. Now it is my firm belief that in order to be the best medium we can be, we must be happy and at one with self.

I was experiencing this brand-new feeling of love that I had never felt before - it felt alien to me! I could now truly understand the pain people felt when they lost their love of a lifetime. When you are training as a medium, a lot of emphasis is put on making loving connections and really connecting with the unconditional love of the spirit world. For the first time in my adult life, I could truly understand what this meant, and in turn with empathy and understanding of real love, I was able to connect with spirit people in a completely different way, often being moved very deeply with the reading I was conducting. Nicky didn't know it, but she was helping develop a fundamental part of mediumship - unconditional love. I couldn't have asked for a better life, and it felt like a magical reward from the spirit world for all of my hard work and dedication. There were so many signs and synchronicities, like the fact Jim had met his wife at the Palais de Danse some 50 years before. I was truly loving myself in the fullest way, I had spent the last 5 years trying to love myself, but I didn't know that in order to really come into my own as a medium I needed the love of another person.

However, even at this point I felt that I wasn't good enough to be a medium! I was so young and was still viewed as just a young laddie, many people couldn't see the vast experience I had, but did people expect too much or was my expectation too much? What was a medium and did people really understand this fully?

Love is such a powerful force. It's there for everyone to embrace - that kind of unconditional love for all of humankind. That is the kind of love that impels people to go into the community and try to change conditions for others, to take risks for what they believe in.

Coretta Scott King

Chapter 5
The wonderful role of a Medium

Isn't it fascinating how we want things quickly and don't give much thought on the journey because we are so focused on the destination? My journey to being a medium was one of frustration at the beginning, I wanted to be good really quickly and by good, I mean giving accurate readings that are accepted by the sitter. I'd like to break this down so it's easier to understand.

When I properly started working as a medium, I was 16 years old, and with what felt like a lifetime of experience before that in my childhood. The truth was that I was very inexperienced, and the things I had to learn first were the life lessons of empathy, understanding, care, and compassion. What is the role of a medium? The role of a medium is to prove the survival of the human soul beyond reasonable doubt. That's it. However, in my eyes, the role of a medium is also so much more. The role of a medium is to facilitate healing between the two worlds by proving survival with evidential mediumship. To expand on this, the role of a medium, as I mentioned before, is also to be the best version of themselves they can be - physically, emotionally, and spiritually. My view on this has stayed the same throughout the years, but sadly I have not always had positive experiences of other people within the spiritual community during my time as a working medium. One thing that has always been clear to me is that we never truly know each person's journey, their story is their own and if we are to make judgement on others then we are not fully embracing our true role as a medium.

I have always promised the spirit world that I would be empathetic, caring, compassionate, and understanding with anyone who chose to sit with me and connect with their loved ones in the spirit world. Often people will call themselves spiritual, but what does that actually mean? Being spiritual is synonymous with being a person whose highest priority is to be loving to yourself and others. For me it was easy to be loving to others but like many others, I was not always loving to myself. I was aware that if I was truly spiritual that I had to be loving to myself and so I needed to work on myself. So, I spoke to myself with kindness every day and learned to truly love the skin I was in. My amazing relationship with my wife also helped me to be that best version of myself, I knew that to be the medium I could be was to highly prioritise loving myself and others. Many mediums talk of ego and how important it is not to have an ego. I had spent a good 5 or 6 years loving myself to then be told I had too much ego from a well-respected medium - who was a teacher within the governing body of mediums. I was upset and a little unsure of why she felt this about me, because I respected her a lot, in fact, I had her on a pedestal. Her words stuck with me, and this led me to research what ego was. You see, I needed to find out what exactly the ego was because at that time, I felt I needed to be able to defend myself with facts. The word ego means a person's sense of self-esteem or self-importance. Of course, we all need some ego otherwise how on earth would we function? Being egotistical on the other hand is often defined as the need to maintain favourable views of oneself, as well as enhance them. Often someone egotistical will have an inflated opinion of themself and place importance on their own amplified vision of themselves.

Once knowing this I felt I was able to defend myself, that I was certainly not egotistical but in fact loving myself, which in turn was the definition of being spiritual. I took this information to her because I felt it was important that she understood ego is a part of self-worth and not necessarily a bad thing. This was a single moment in time that encouraged me to make a promise to the spirit world and myself that if I was ever to teach mediumship that I would help people who were spiritual to embrace that wonderful gift of self-worth and help to develop the ego to be more aware of being spiritual. I hope by writing this book it inspires mediums, teachers, and anyone to trust that yes, you need ego. It is part of your human right to feel you have importance to this world but never to tip over that edge and think you are more important than anyone else by becoming egotistical. So, for those 5 years I spent so much time understanding and loving myself, and at the time by truly loving myself, it helped me to move out of a difficult relationship and months later meet my amazing wife. When we align ourselves with who we are then miracles can happen.

There have been times in my journey as a medium where my mediumship has been mediocre to say the least and on reflection these times were times where I wasn't looking after myself. Looking after ourselves physically, emotionally, and spiritually is vital to our human and mediumistic development and when one of these elements is out of sync, everything falls apart. If you aren't comfortable with yourself and have feelings of loathing and hating yourself emotionally, physically, or spiritually - how on earth can you be a kind caring and empathetic medium? How we live as people absolutely determines how we connect as mediums. The way I look at this is that if I were in the spirit world and wanted to pass on to my family, I was okay, I would choose a medium who was kind, caring, empathetic and felt good about themselves, so as the message they passed on was honest and good and had no ulterior motive. The word medium itself means halfway between two extremes. So, a medium who feels good about themselves has the ability to truly move past their own thoughts and judgements, and step back to truly work from a place of impartiality. If you ever hear a medium talk about another medium's work, my advice is to walk away and don't work with them. They need to heal something within themself and maybe they are not in the best place to give you a reading. Interpreting your own energy and being aware of your own self and senses is often a skill missed by even the happiest, most balanced human beings on the planet.

Transformation is a journey without a destination, the Dragonfly trusts the process of metamorphosis without thinking of the destination.

The Soul Man

Finding the Medium Within You - 3

To understand our own energy, we must first understand personal responsibility. To understand personal responsibility then the first thing that every working medium must realise is that they have a massive responsibility to look after themselves. But what does this mean? When we are working with a vulnerable, grieving person it is almost impossible to work from a place of genuine empathy, care and understanding if we don't feel that way about ourselves. Just like my story of meeting my wife, she showed me true love which helped me become the best medium I can be. If you're developing as a medium but talk badly about yourself such as "I'm too fat, I'm not good enough" etc then you are essentially lowering your vibration and thinking too much. This means you aren't able to access the superconscious because instead of feeling, you are too much in your thoughts. The same can be said for commenting negatively on social media, talking badly about others and so on. You are coming from a critical and unkind place, and just like your visible reputation, your invisible reputation also precedes you. I know if I passed into the spirit world tomorrow, I would seek a medium to represent me who was kind and compassionate and had done lots of emotional and physical work on themselves. I would want someone who would talk positively to my family, removing their own feelings and thoughts, and become my words, my feelings, my love.

Personally, I am always working on myself, trying every day to be a better person than I was yesterday. As I mentioned before, a medium's job is to prove the existence of the human soul beyond reasonable doubt and be the best version of themself spiritually, physically, and emotionally. How and who you are as a person directly influences your connection with the spirit world. Being a medium and giving that proof comes with significant responsibility, and a medium should be able to understand someone's emotional state of mind. Many times, I have sat with someone who simply should not have a reading. If someone is suffering from poor emotional wellbeing and they come for a reading it can be the most destructive thing in the world. If someone is inebriated or under the influence of drugs it can also be extremely destructive because their inhibitions are heightened, and they aren't thinking rationally. A medium or psychic can be the first person someone sees when they are in crisis and that is an important thing to bear in mind. Some people would rather see us than speak to a health professional, and that is why it is essential that anyone doing this work has some basic, but preferably extended, knowledge and understanding on how to help people who aren't well. Of course, we cannot diagnose but we can stop the reading and signpost them to a helpful organisation, charity or even encourage them to make a call to their GP. I would love to have every single working medium on the planet trained in mental health first aid or at least have some understanding of this and how to help people.

With this in mind, I would like to introduce you to the wonderful LEAF Approach. This will help you in developing the relationships you have with everyone around you including the spirit world.

People won't always remember what you say but they remember how you make them feel. Can you think of a time when someone has made you feel a certain way? What did they say to you? Can't remember? You won't recall the exact words they said but I bet you remember how they made you feel. People and human behaviour fascinate me, I don't believe there's inherently good or bad people, I believe we just make conscious choices based on our experiences. Our behaviour is almost always defined by how we respond to the things around us. We all face numerous occasions on a regular basis which feel stressful, chaotic, and conflicting but it is how we respond to them that matters most. What do people need when they are acting from a place of fear/frustration/anger? What do you need in these situations? UNDERSTANDING and EMPATHY. We can be quick to judge someone's behaviour or even our own, so when you can remove yourself from that and focus on understanding why with compassion and care, it changes the whole situation.

Liz was a lady I worked with for many years, Liz was the grumpy one in the office known for her grumpy attitude, nobody asked Liz for anything because she would say no. Liz sat on her own for break times and seldom came to team nights out. That was the story I was told about Liz but using my intense empathy I wanted to know why. I felt sorry for Liz, I hadn't had a chance to speak to Liz because initially I believed the story that was told to me by others. One day during the working week, I was in the local Tesco for my lunch and Liz popped into my head. I decided that I had to get a box of chocolates and a card, so that's just what I did! I wrote in the card "Just a wee note to say I care. Lots of love Steven" and placed it on her desk along with the chocolates. Liz came back from her work, and she looked at the card, however, to my disappointment she stuck the card back in the envelope and then left early that day. At the time I thought how ungrateful she was, but how wrong I was to judge. Just like how I spoke earlier about the flowers, giving something for my own gratification will never work, I had to give without expecting anything in return and change my attitude. Liz came back to work the following day and came in early, she walked straight towards me and sat down by my desk, "Steven, I just wanted to say thank you for the lovely gift, I didn't think anyone liked me in this place." At that moment, I realised that I had made an assumption based on everyone else's experience and not looked at the situation with understanding and empathy. This was the last time I would ever make an assumption about anyone. After that, Liz spoke to me often and others would never understand our friendship because they didn't take the time to listen.

My understanding of Liz was part of the LEAF Approach. Let's look at the LEAF Approach, it will transform every conversation you have! This concept is something I have created from my experience working as a manager of people over the years and observing others and their interactions. The LEAF Approach combines the different skills and techniques I have learnt through my own practice on getting the most from everyday interactions with others and helping each other to have calm and kind conversations.

L isten

I had to listen to what was happening here. Listening is more than using your ears, it's about feeling the energy of the room and paying attention to what your body and gut instinct is telling you. I could see Liz was uncomfortable, I listened to the room by observing everyone's body language - the way they spoke and acted. Using silence instead of filling silences with words that don't matter.

When I use silence, people have space to talk. For example, someone might say "I'm going through such a hard time at the moment", I pause, and I reply, "what do you think you need to do?" Then I stay silent to let them talk, this silence gives them space to find the answer, the space to deep dive into their subconscious where the answers reside. It's very empowering for the other person.

In the case of Liz, I said to her "what makes you think nobody likes you?" Then I gave SILENCE. Liz found the answer herself.

E mpathise

Showing genuine empathy and being truly fascinated by what is going on behind someone's behaviour is a real skill. It takes a lot of practice to really take away any judgement you may have. I see people acting in ways that could be seen as bad, ignorant, or anger fuelled, and I think "what course of events has led you to acting the way you do? What has hurt you?" Usually when someone is acting in this way the first thing I say is "are you okay?" Then I use silence (back to Listen) and the silence can often be long! Usually people react one of two ways, they get upset because someone is showing care, or they get defensive. Usually when they get defensive it is because something in us is leaking out, perhaps a frustration of ours with the way they are acting. The way to get past this is having the right attitude!

A ttitude

How is your attitude? Your attitude is how you think or feel about something and if someone is acting in a way that's difficult then it is not easy to change your attitude, especially when you have always had a different approach in the past. Maybe in the past you have responded with a frustrated attitude - how dare they speak to you like that? Changing that attitude to one of acceptance and understanding can change everything. With Liz, my attitude had to be one of complete understanding and no judgement otherwise she would have felt instantly that I wasn't interested. Take some time to think about your attitude when dealing with difficult people! Do you come from a place of acceptance and kindness, or do you come from a place of judgement and criticism? It's hard to do but once you see it, you will start checking yourself all the time and thinking very carefully about everything you say to people, and how you respond to all different scenarios with your friends, family, and strangers.

F eel /fix

Feel and fix is the one part of the Leaf approach that is all up to you. Remember you cannot fix people, but you can inspire them to open up through kindness and compassion, listening and understanding with bags of empathy and lots of silence.

You cannot change a person but by showing empathy, you can make them think and feel deeply and drive connection. Human beings need connection, it is vital to our survival. We need to feel loved and there's not a single person on the planet who doesn't want to be liked.

Exercise: Write down the name of someone you'd like to use the leaf approach with:

- How will you listen?
- Empathise etc?
- Have the right attitude?
- Help them feel or fix?
- What might be going on with them?
- Why do they feel or think that certain way?

Judging a person does not define who they are…it defines who you are.

Unknown

Chapter 6
Ability

What is reading people in mediumship? Does anyone know what that actually means? The truth is that reading means many things. Most mediums work on recommendations, this means clients they have read for will recommend them to others, but is there understanding as to what that reading would involve prior to the reading taking place? My understanding when I'm reading is that I am reading and interpreting the energies used by the spirit world in order to understand the message they are trying to convey. It may surprise you to know that over the years and the thousands of people I have sat with every single communication is different.

We all have five senses as humans - smell, sight, taste, touch, and hearing. Some people talk about people having a sixth sense and they are right to an extent, but when we look at it there is so much more:

Clairvoyance, the ability to see clearly in the mind's eye.
Clairaudience the ability to hear clearly what the ears cannot.
Clairgustance the ability to taste without food or drink.
Clairsentience the ability to feel energy unseen and unheard by the normal five senses.
Clairscent the ability to smell a scent without a clear physical source of that scent near you.

There are many others but these are the main senses.

So, you see, a medium works within all of these senses and will not just be clairvoyant or just clairsentient, they use a range of them combined. If they didn't, that would be a little like saying you can drive a car just relying on your sense of smell!

Clairvoyance is like daydreaming. It isn't always necessarily seeing dead folk walking around the place, it is way more subtle than that, for example, seeing an image of someone in your mind that you have no previous recollection of. Let's try a quick exercise here. I'd like you to think about your mother, see her face, her eyes, what is she wearing? The texture of her skin really builds up a mental picture of her. Now what you're doing is just like clairvoyance, you have your eyes open and are able to see in what's called your mind's eye the person you are thinking of. You are activating your visual cortex to have the ability to see the person. Now I can hear you saying "yeah, yeah that's just your imagination." For most, yeah that's the case but for mediums it's very different. We rely on our visual cortex to be able to describe to a person the physical description of a person. Can you imagine seeing the spirit world walking around the place with your physical sense of sight? I can tell you it is not nice, and most mediums choose not to see spirit in this way. Of course, when we are young, and at points through our life, we will see spirit as solid apparitions, but for most part we will see spirit clairvoyantly meaning seeing without the eyes.

I cannot remember my first experience with clairvoyant sight but the first time I remember really seeing in my mind's eyes with intention was that time in bed/crib when I was a baby seeing my ancestors all around me. So, to answer the question about conjuring an image in your mind's imagination, the answer is yes. However, to a medium we allow the space in our mind to clear and without thinking of someone we know, we allow the spirit world to filter in and show us the way they looked when they were alive. In my experience they always show themselves younger, usually at a point we remember them. Now who wouldn't show themself younger? I certainly will. This is a fundamental skill of evidence-based mediumship, the ability to prove the person's likeness without having known the person.

So, what about the other senses? Clairsentience - knowing. This is a strong feeling within me telling me what I know. To add to this, we may whilst connecting, smell certain scents or feel different emotions or perhaps see other things as well as the person, this is all of the psychic senses working together to give evidence-based mediumship.

I experienced all of these senses together on one occasion when I was a teenager again in the wee hours between midnight to 5am. I was around 17 and my family had all gone to bed as they usually did, Mum and Dad in the room just off my box room and my sister in the front room of the house. Much like the time when I had seen my Grandad, I woke to find a small older lady standing by the side of the bed, she was around 5ft, slender build with white hair and really prominent eyes. She looked familiar but I didn't know who she was. I've spoken about the clair senses but sometimes we experience things with our physical senses as well as the spiritual senses, and on this occasion, I was most definitely experiencing things physically. "STEVEN" she said whilst shaking me back and forth, "GO WAKE UP YOUR MUM" she had an urgency in her voice. I should have been concerned with who she was but instead I leapt up out of bed and rushed to my Mum's room. I couldn't see her, she didn't seem to be in her room, "MUM" I shouted but she didn't answer. I ran downstairs to see if she was there and she wasn't, she was out. The strange thing was that her car keys were still there hanging in the kitchen. I went back to bed in my sleepy state thinking nothing more of what had just happened. Then before I knew it, I was being shaken again "STEVEN, I need you to go wake your Mum up before it's too late". Admittedly, this time I'm less enthusiastic, but I got up to go check on my Mum. This time I saw that my Mum was there but was lying very still, her bedroom was taken up by her double bed, mirrored wardrobes to the left of the bed and the green glow from her alarm clock illuminated the room. "MUM" I said as I shook her like the old lady had shaken me moments before. She wasn't waking up, was limp, and lifeless, "MUM" I shouted again.

What was going on? Surely, she wasn't dead! I kept thinking that I can't lose my Grandad and my Mum! My memory flicked back to that cold night in November 5 years beforehand where I found my Grandad. The stillness and the pause in time all felt too relevant! I could feel the woman behind me again pushing me and telling me to wake her up. This time not hearing her with my ears but internally and knowing how urgent this was becoming. I shook my Mum really hard and, in that moment, she sat up poker straight and inhaled a massive breath, almost like she had been underwater and taking that much needed gasp of oxygen! She looked really startled and time began to tick again, my Dad who had obviously been sleeping woke to tell me to go back to bed! So, I went back to bed thinking what the hell was that all about? In the morning I reminded Mum of what had happened the night before and she was so surprised. "Steven, I need to tell you what happened to me" she said, "I was with your Grandad in this wonderful peaceful place, I had no stress, no worries, I felt completely at peace. Grandad was introducing me to all of these family members I had never met. It was so nice to spend time with him again, I could really feel him there! Then he told me to go back and gently pushed me back. I could hear your voice shouting "MUM", but I didn't want to come with you. I wanted to stay with my Dad, he kept pushing me back until I woke up with you in front of me! I believe I visited heaven and you brought me back."

I'm so grateful that this lady came to warn me that Mum needed to be brought back. I believe that when presented with the choice to stay in the spirit world most people would choose to stay there because of this intense feeling of love that it delivers us. All these years have passed, and I still didn't have a clue who that lady was until recently. What I was about to find out at the age of 37 was mind blowing and I couldn't quite believe the proof I was about to be submitted with. My Granny had been keeping really unwell and my Mum wanted to make her feel better, so she reached out to my great auntie to ask if she had any old photos of my Granny's mother. You see, her mum had passed away when my Granny was 12 and she hadn't seen a photograph of her since she passed away. To my Mum's surprise, my auntie had more than one photo; she had a photo of not only her mother, my great grandmother, but one of her and my great great grandmother too. My Mum surprised my Granny with the photos and filmed her whilst showing Granny the photos, so we were all able to join in on this special moment to see her emotional reaction after all this time. I asked my Mum if I could see the photo, and when she handed me the photo, my eyes almost popped out of my head. It was the woman who shook me to wake me! She had passed away some 40-50 years before I was even born. The lady who woke me was my great, great grandmother.

Let's talk about the other senses:

Clairaudience is hearing an internal voice that is not your own. This sense is not always necessarily hearing someone talking directly into your ear, however I have heard voices directly on many occasions. However, can you imagine walking around your everyday life hearing and seeing people not of this world? For myself, that would really disturb me.

Clairgustance is when we are able to taste our granny's tablet, or mince and potatoes, even when she's no longer able to cook physical food. Usually, I will get the taste of someone's favourite food (usually cake) which is great confirmation to the person I'm reading.

Clairsentience is usually something I experience more psychically with physical people, you just feel their energy and are able to tap into their feelings, emotions, and physical wellbeing. It works the same with the spirit world when it comes to giving evidence of the feelings they had in the body before they passed to spirit.

Clairscent is a smell and I guess perhaps one of the clearest senses for me, I often smell cigarette smoke, perfumes, or someone's natural aroma. Do you ever get a smell and it just transports you back to a time, a place, or a person? That's what clairscent is like.

One of our greatest gifts is our intuition. It's a sense we all have...we just need to learn to tap into and trust it.

Donna Karan

Finding the Medium Within You - 4

We have spoken about the senses, the subconscious and superconscious, and the LEAF Approach, but how do we take our awareness from the conscious mind to the subconscious and superconscious? The answer is meditation! The word meditation means to ponder so with a practice of meditation we are able to alter our conscious state and ponder on the space between our thoughts, the superconscious. Many spiritualist churches have what are called open awareness circles in which they sit as a group for usually around an hour pondering on a connection with the spirit world and pushing out their own consciousness to connect. This wasn't enough for me, one hour simply wouldn't be enough, I needed to immerse myself in this altered state and nobody could ever really explain what it was. You just meditate and information comes to you, so I ventured on my own journey to discover what meditation was and how I could use it to further develop my mediumship.

Meditation helps us to slow down our brain waves and access the subconscious mind and then the superconscious with prolonged focus. When we are experiencing stress, our sympathetic nervous system kicks in, releasing stress hormones that help you either run or fight back. Once the danger has passed, your parasympathetic nervous system activates and allows you to rest and relax. During meditation you are constantly tapping into the parasympathetic nervous system, and as the body fully relaxes the spirit world is then able to tap into our soft relaxed energy. What is fascinating about meditation is that there is a huge increase in serotonin, the feel-good chemical allowing us to feel a sense of wellbeing. Meditation reduces cortisol levels and the stress hormones in the body allowing us to feel much less stressed, which was something I found I got a lot of with my regular practice. Meditation also increases levels of melatonin, the sleep hormone, another great way to connect with the subconscious, and also to get a wonderful night's sleep. There are so many more benefits of the chemical response of meditation but most of all meditation can reduce perceived stress massively as well as helping us connect with the superconscious.

My advice to anyone wishing to start a connection with spirit is to form some sort of meditation practice. I have meditated daily for just 10 minutes every single day for the last 25 years. Meditation can also provide you with the perfect opportunity to move into the superconscious in a much more profound way which I'll speak about later.

Meditation is being in tune with our inner universe.

Unknown

Chapter 7
My amazing Granny

My dearest Granny Helen was one of the most wonderful ladies that walked the planet, a tenacious driven lady that inspired me to work hard my whole life and never give up on my dreams. I have never met such a hard-working lady. When I was around eight years old my Granny would have been only forty-three years old so was in the prime of her life and had so much energy and tenacity. Granny was never unwell in her life other than her asthma she was a very active, fit and mentally determined person.

As I start to write this part of the book, I am actually sitting here in the hospital ward with her.

My beloved Granny, Helen, lies in her hospital bed in the last hours and minutes of her life. I look at her and understand in that moment the frailty of life.

The lady I always looked at as the strong one was now so weak and unable to communicate. When you're sitting with someone at the end of life many things go through your head; the memories that you held together and the realisation that their physical being is about to be no longer. What would life be like without my Granny? She was the only grandmother I had ever known as my Dad's mother wasn't really around when we were little. I love my Granny so much and my heart hurts at the thought of her physical self not being here. No more kisses, no more cuddles and long chats with her. She was about to be part of the spirit world and I knew my job here was to prepare her for her transition, you see she was absolutely terrified to die!

My Granny and I had many conversations over the years about the afterlife, she did not quite understand the experiences I had as a child but was always very supportive and never judged. The afterlife was terrifying and fascinating for her, and I could feel her energy deep within her body experiencing that fear as she was no longer able to communicate with us. She had had around 30 heart attacks in the last few months and was in hospital being monitored. I would go and visit, and she would sit moaning about everyone in the ward much to my amusement, she was definitely honest, that's for sure. The nursing team all knew her well and were always so good to her. I felt really bad as I couldn't always get over to see her, but she would always say "listen ma darlin' you are a busy man, I understand". This time Granny's hospital stay was expected to end a few days later and she would return home to be looked after by my amazing Mum who did everything for her. My Mum called me about 7pm on a Thursday evening worried that this time things didn't look good, Granny had taken a turn for the worst. I looked at my wife sitting on the other end of the couch and told her "I think this is it Nicky, I think Granny is on her way." "GO!" she said, and I threw on a pair of shoes and drove the 2-minute drive to the hospital. I ran through the hospital corridors to get to her side, I knew I would be first there out of the family due to my closeness to the hospital. She couldn't go on her own. "Don't you bloody take her!" I shouted to the invisible army now surrounding me. I got to the ward and could see her at the end of the ward through the curtain. She was screaming and clearly terrified as I got into the room. I held her hand and said "Granny, Granny, it's Steven". She instantly calmed down. The nursing team gave her meds and oxygen, and there she lay for 4 days and 4 nights. The whole family gathered around her, but I never left her side and when I did only to sleep in the knowledge someone else was with her, I would not let her pass on her own.

My Granny had lost my Grandad, John, five years ago almost to the day. He had cancer. Even to his very last day here on earth he did not want to accept that he had limited time and my Granny also did not want to accept that he had limited time. After his passing, she was comforted in the fact that each time I went to visit I would feel his presence in the room and the house. He was everywhere. Granny tried so hard to feel him but could not and this upset her because she really wanted to feel him in the room with her. As it happened, in the last year or so of her life she was very aware of my Grandad's presence, so much so in fact that she had many dreams about him she felt his energy in the room. She told my Mum, my sister and I about how she knew that the afterlife was real.

It is a really strange thing to be sitting in a hospital side ward and seeing everyone else go around their daily business. The nurses and the visitors all hopeful that their loved ones will get home. As I sit here now, I know that my Granny will not be coming home. Not in the way that we would like her to. I am comforted by the knowledge that her dad, her brothers, and my Grandad will be waiting for her as she makes her transition to the spirit world. I wonder as I stare at my Granny gasping and holding onto her breaths, "can you hear me? Are you aware of what's going on?" I ask her "Granny can you hear me?" I get no response, not a squeeze of the hand, not even a wink of the eye, but today is unlike any other day. You see, the other days we visited her in the hospital there was almost an urgency within her, I felt her energy urgent to get back to her conscious waking life, but not today. It feels as though she's slipping between the two worlds, and deep down I know this is the truth. I can feel the energy of the room, there's a calmness that has come across her, it's tangible and it's comforting. This is the first time that I have sat with someone at the end of life who is as close as my Granny is to me. My Granny is like my Mum to me. She was that lady in my life who was always there, always close, and the person I could tell anything to. There was no judgement, only love, care, and compassion.

We spent a lot of time at my Granny's house when we were little, she was a very active lady who was the housekeeper for Major Kenneth Scott, the owner of Cakemuir Castle near Pathhead. Granny's cottage was part of the castle estate, and we grew up running down the halls of this amazing building. When you entered the castle through the main door there was a small seating area with wellie boots and a gun room to the right with a large moose head mounted to the wall which we called 'Monty'. To the left was a glass door leading to Major Scott's desk which led to French doors taking you to the back garden. The back garden was grand and well kept, all of the gardens were about the size of three football pitches and looked like a scene from the television show, Downton Abbey. To the left of the glass entry door there was a spiral staircase with a thick piece of rope hanging from the centre, "Hello" my Granny would shout up the stairs to the library where Major Scott would sit with his morning paper. "Hello Helen" he would reply, and we would then walk up the stairs to speak with him. The library was a large square room with two sofas positioned in an L shape in front of a grand fireplace with familiar looking logs from our logging adventures in a wicker basket by the fire. Around the library were bookcases about 3 feet tall around every wall in the room. There were only four of us there, my Granny, my sister, Major Scott, and I, but it felt like so many more.

It is only now that I realise that in walking the halls of this castle that I always felt that it was full of people that other people could not see. My Granny always had a busy day from cleaning the castle, which was massive, to cooking the meals and setting the fires for the evening. My sister and I had the run of the whole place and Major Scott was happy for us to play wherever we liked as long as we didn't break anything. It was like stepping back to the 1940s, it would be strange to see a modern telephone or TV in certain rooms as the rest of the castle was set in a time warp. As I walked through the many rooms, my mind would stick in the superconscious, seeing and feeling the many people who had visited including Mary Queen of Scots and Robert the Bruce who have connections with the castle, their statues immortalising their stays in the grounds at the front of the building. I would sit in the playroom and feel the energy of things that had happened in that room, not necessarily of the souls of the deceased but of the residual energy left over in the room. Every room had a different person and a different story. I was very aware of the fact that it was once a busy home with many staff looking after its occupants and Major Scott was only part of the history. For a young medium this was such an enriching experience, I was getting to experience this amazing haunted old castle with no prior knowledge. Much of what I experienced was backed up by Major Scott as we sat for lunch in the grand kitchen. At lunch time my Granny would cook a wonderful meal on the Aga and the table was fully set, Major Scott would have the job of preparing the diluted orange juice as we sat awaiting lunch. After we had eaten, I would tell him about who I thought had stayed in the castle and he was always able to confirm, and I was pleased that he could confirm. However, it was just confirmation, I didn't need validation and I was never shocked or surprised. That was until the lady in the red dress.

I would see the lady in the red dress at the top of the old wooden staircase that led up to Major Scott's bedroom, she would stand and stare. She always looked so lovely and radiated kindness, I was never afraid of her. She told me that her dresses were kept in one of the cupboards at the top of the stairs. One lunchtime, I asked Major Scott who owned the dresses at the top of the stairs, he choked up a little and told me to finish my food. He then sat and stared into space for 10 minutes. Granny was giving me the eyes, you know when you are in trouble and the eyes swell like bulging light bulbs! I knew to keep my mouth shut at this point. "Those dresses belonged to Lady Scott, young man. She was a wonderful kind lady, she was my wife, and she is now in heaven". "No she isn't!" I said. My Granny was now morphing into a puffer fish!
"But I have seen her" I said.
"Have you?" he replied.
"Yes and she's very nice".
"I have seen her too, young man, thank you for letting me know, now it's time to retire to the library" and he left the room. Granny gave me a telling off and told me not to be so outspoken.

I have always been able to sense energy, not always ghosts as people might think but just the energy of things that have happened in a certain place. Going to Granny's was always a special experience not just because we got to go to work with her but also because Granny taught me how to bake, she taught me how to cook and how to show your family love by bringing them round the table and feeding them amazing food. I think back on all of these memories and experiences as I sit here in this hospital room with her. Granny was the oldest sister of four boys and four girls, all of her brothers would spend the summer at the castle estate chopping down trees in the nearby forest and turning them into logs during the logging season. We have really many fond memories of this because the whole family would come together to log the trees, and then eat, drink and be merry afterwards! These are really happy memories when she was such a vibrant person bringing her family together. Seeing my Granny as she lies in this hospital bed today, alone with all of those brothers in the spirit world, and I wonder, even though it is not in my awareness, are they here? Are they waiting for her? Are they helping her with her transition between the two worlds? Why am I not seeing this, why am I not able to experience this transition? Maybe it is not for me to see, maybe, just maybe I am to help her from this side of life, and it is their job to help her from that side of life. Maybe I am just not meant to see that.

I spend the whole day by my Granny's side with my laptop, thinking about the words that I am going to write at this moment. The nurses come in and I tell them what I am doing, they find it very comforting, and they are excited to read the finished content. My Granny was a regular visitor to this ward in the hospital and the nursing staff loved her, especially one member of staff whose name escapes me, but I remember the kindness that she showed my Granny in these last hours of her life. She had come in about five o'clock and said, "we're just going to give Helen a washdown and get her nice and comfortable and check her medication." My Mum and I both agreed and decided to go for a walk but if anything changed to call us. On the walk I said to my Mum that I thought that when we go back in, Granny is going to let go, that I could feel her energy draining from this side of life. My Mum was hesitant and disagreed, however, I realised that Granny needed something from my Mum. I said "Mum, you need to give her permission to leave. She needs to know that it's okay to go." When we went back into the hospital room, they had given my Granny a wash, put her favourite blanket over her and the lovely nurse had sprayed some of my Granny's favourite perfume.

I played on my phone the song that I had played at my Grandad's funeral - Cilla Black 'I Only Love To Love You'. In those moments we could feel her energy slipping away more and more. I said to my Mum "it's important now that you give her permission", so my Mum reached over, held her hand and said to her Mum "it's okay to go now, go get him, John's waiting for you." The track changed to Cilla Black 'You're My World' and almost on cue to the chorus line 'you're my world, your every breath' she seemed to take her last breaths. My Mum panicked and got the nurse, but I stayed and held her hand. The nurse came back in and said, "no she's not quite away yet, hold her hand". My Mum held her hand and she slipped gently into the spirit world.

Now what is strange for me is that in these moments I thought I was going to see a light, feel all the people around the bed and have a spiritual experience. But I didn't. I was very consciously aware I was not allowed to see this part, that I was only allowed to be the person to help her to pass. We sat with my Granny for a while until my sister and my uncle came to see their goodbyes and in the hour that passed by, I had the strangest feeling of peace as they sat and stared at her body, feeling the emptiness that lay in front of me. That vibrant amazing person she was, was no longer in front of me. She was part of something greater now, something that is beyond most human understanding. It is a scientific fact that energy cannot be destroyed, it merely changes, and this is something I have been aware of my whole life. My amazing Granny was now part of that evolutionary change that we must all experience in this lifetime. She was finally with my Grandad who she had missed so much, and I felt so glad for her that she was now by his side.

After her passing, I thought I would sense her around me. She was such an important person in my life, and I wanted to feel her energy. However, the weeks passed by, and I thought to myself, why am I not feeling her around me? Why haven't I had a visit from her yet?

It wasn't until I was doing a therapy called Baud Therapy with my friend Susan whilst in my shop that I had my first experience of my Granny's energy. Baud Therapy requires you to concentrate on something that has been traumatic, and the equipment helps to distort that traumatic event. For me, it had quite the opposite effect, as it put me immediately into a different level of consciousness: the superconscious. I found myself standing in a meeting place between the two worlds – physical and spirit - and smiling at me from the side of the room was my Granny and my Grandad. They were a much younger version of my Granny and Grandad, and in that moment, I knew it was them. They didn't need to speak any words; I could feel their happiness and that was enough for me.

As I was growing up, something that I could always feel in the room between my Granny and Grandad was how much my Grandad adored my Granny, and vice versa. I know that the love and the nurture that I was given as a child has made me the very best medium today. You can't teach love and compassion, they are things that must come naturally from someone, and I believe that to work with the spirit world it is essential that we have love and compassion. As I have said earlier, if I were in the spirit world and I wanted someone to pass on messages to my loved ones, I would want that person to be someone who is kind and caring and who would do it responsibly. It really is a strange thing when someone that you loved so much passes to the spirit world. I asked my Granny to promise me if she could come back and give me evidence that she was ok. I thought that she would do that pretty quickly, however, as I am writing this sometime after she passed, she has not connected to me directly. What has happened is that she has used all of the amazing people that I work with to get her messages across. She is always hanging around my shop and always giving people messages that she is there looking after me and so proud of me just like she was in life.

Losing my Granny has helped give me understanding and empathy for others who have lost their grandmothers. I guess times like this really make us question everything around us - why my Granny? Why from everyone in the world did my Granny have to pass? Why can't I see sense and feel her when others can? Since she has passed, I've had so many people say to me, "yeah but you are lucky Steven you can see the spirit world". And so, I want to go into this a little bit more and help you to understand that as mediums we feel the love of our family around us, but we seldom get to see them and speak to them the same way we can with other peoples loved ones. The answer is clear to me, that we don't really need the validation as we know they are okay, and we question any possible connection we make with our loved ones as our imagination because we want to connect so badly. Nothing beats just standing there, going about your daily life, and feeling that love connect with you again. As I sit here now, I feel my Granny's hands on my shoulders observing the words, she makes me feel safe and is encouraging me to keep writing, just like she would do in life. I feel her words "you can do anything you put your mind to ma darlin." Even feeling this, I question it - is it my imagination? No, it's not, she is here.

Remember ma darlin' you are special. You are important in this world, one day you'll be on stage sharing who you are with the world, and I'll be there with you… Never forget that.

Helen Rodger (Steven's Granny)

Chapter 8
Evidence

One of the best, most exciting experiences as a medium was my first ever public demonstration in Albany Street. I was 16 years old, and I stood at the lectern for the very first time. I looked out at the audience and thought *oh my god what am I doing here?* I had this amazing trust in the spirit world that they would always show up, and I guess I've had that trust in them from the very beginning. However, I realise now that I had imposter syndrome, something that I have always struggled with my whole life, especially if I was standing on the platform where many famous mediums had stood before. It is a strange thing standing there and not quite understanding where you fit. I guess the role of a medium is always to be that go between, but people look at you like you are some kind of superhuman being. As I stood there on that first day looking out at the audience, my whole world came down to that moment in time where I closed my eyes and put all my trust in the spirit world. I could feel them gathering around me in the same way that I would watch other mediums as they closed their eyes to connect. Closing my eyes is probably one of the greatest gifts in my mediumship and the reason being is it is because when I close my eyes it helps me to disconnect from what I am seeing in front of me and just completely trust. As I stood there welcoming in the spirit world, I could feel the energy of all of the mediums that stood there before me. An army of mediums willing to support me in every single way possible, you see in the world of mediumship we should all be helping each other, and I was certainly getting lots and lots of help from the mediums who had walked this platform before me. It really was the greatest privilege.

When I was a little boy, my Granny always said that I would be on stage, and here was my chance. It was my turn to prove the survival of the human soul, it was my turn to do it my way. I guess it's really easy to fall into the trap of imitating other mediums and that's not something I ever wanted to do. I always wanted to do this my way. I always wanted to be a unique medium with a unique way of working. I stood there that day and the messages I gave to the congregation were the most amazing evidence of survival after physical death. I stepped down from the platform after delivering my evidence and strangely enough the one thing that I was most concerned about was did I say the prayer correctly. I came away from the platform with complete trust that everything that I had just delivered in my mediumship was correct.

My next notable experience of imposter syndrome was when I sat in the chair in the private reading room. This was the chair that Mary Duffy had sat in to deliver her readings. Mary Duffy was a very well-known medium and had passed away earlier that year. I will never forget this reading, it was a lady who had seen me working on the public platform and she had asked for a private reading with me. The private reading felt much more difficult to wrap my head around purely and simply because it was so intense, it was just me and this little lady in a room. I had the massive responsibility of connecting her with someone she desperately wanted to hear from. From my experience, people don't give that much thought about the responsibility of a medium, it really is a huge and significant thing. Can you imagine sitting waiting for information to pass on to someone and every single word that passes your lips is met with great anticipation from the person sitting in front of you? This information has to be absolutely spot-on otherwise what's the point? So, I sat there with this lady and the connection I made was with her husband, an Italian man, who stepped forward and the first clair sense that I was aware of was clair essence: the ability to smell. I said to her that I can smell leather, and did it make sense? She said that it absolutely made complete sense. Then using my very limited knowledge at the time all I could see was a Dolmio advert that was on the TV. The spirit world like to use our experiences of life to share knowledge and understanding and the easiest way for her husband to share who he was with her was to show me the Dolmio advert, so I said to her "do you understand why I am seeing the Dolmio advert?" She started laughing uncontrollably and said, "yes I understand that very well". It turned out not only was her husband Italian, but he also looks like the man from the Dolmio advert! She showed me a picture afterwards to prove this. We went through her session, and I proved to her beyond reasonable doubt that her husband was still very much a part of her life with lots of laughter, tears, and healing. I will never forget this reading because it was the first reading that gave me the confidence to work more closely in the field of private sittings.

But what do I mean when I say *beyond reasonable doubt*? I feel it is very important that when conducting a reading that the conditions are set up in a way that all potential variables of doubt are removed. These are things that may cause the sitter to doubt the ability of the medium and will include the medium having no knowledge of why the person is there. It's important that the medium knows no information about the sitter, and we often say in The Soul Man and Friends to clients "keep us in the dark!" A medium should welcome conditions to work in with no precursors. For myself, I like to close my eyes as I work so I am not looking at the person's reactions to what I say. An example of why this is so important happened very recently, I was sitting conducting a reading with a woman who kept telling me unwanted information, much more than confirmation that either the message I am giving to her is something she can take or not. My job as the medium is to give her the information, and so in this case I told her that we were unable to continue with the reading, because the information she was giving me created reasonable doubt to the communication. The medium should have a blank canvas to work on to avoid doubt being cast on the communication. Proof is always something so important to a medium because we need to prove beyond reasonable doubt that the evidence, we are giving is credible and sometimes that proof is as simple as a word.

Another memorable reading from my early days of mediumship took place again in the same draughty room at Albany Street. I sat in my usual way, asking the spirit world to step closer and help me prove beyond reasonable doubt that they were still part of my sitter's life. In the sitter came and I felt that the energy in the room was full of anticipation. She asked me straightaway "come on then, what do you see?" I closed my eyes and the first image I saw was the Tasmanian devil. Not sure what else to say to her, I opened my eyes and told her "okay erm, well, I see the cartoon character the Tasmanian devil." Her jaw hit the floor and her eyes filled with tears. There was a long pause, after which she laid down money on the small table in front of me beside my jug of water, thanked me and walked out the door. I had no idea what had just happened. We had barely sat together, and I had told her only one thing. It was later that I found out why she had left after that short time. The experience had impacted her so much that she called Albany Street and told the President about a code word with her mother. There was no way that anybody else would know this code word, and she was absolutely gobsmacked by my reading and that was all the proof she needed. The code word she had agreed with her mum should she come back after death was the simple cartoon character of the Tasmanian devil. You see, that's all she needed, she didn't need the screeds of information, she needed the simple code word.

I started to get new clients all the time and bear in mind I was working full time at college, and part-time cleaning in the early mornings for extra income. So, all of my spiritual work was in my spare time. I would often sit in my kitchen doing sittings for my wife's friends and their friends and family and so on. Bringing people and their folk into our home was something really different because this was my own environment, and I was about to learn at the age of 21 just how important these boundaries were. I had a job to fill a gap in employment in a local nursing home. I believe that this was a place I was sent to help souls who were at end of life. It is an experience that changed and developed my whole perception of life and death because before I hadn't really faced physical death other than finding my Grandad that day. I was a carer and I would go in to work at the care home and get residents up from bed, dress them and help with all areas of their daily life. It was hard work and I have so much respect for anyone who does this role.

I had many, many spirit experiences in this place. The first and most memorable experience was a man that I will call George. He was an old man in his 70s who never spoke and only sat in his chair all day looking miserable. He had MRSA and dementia as well as being unable to walk. He would sit in his pyjamas all day which always frustrated me because he has a wardrobe full of clothes. In order to dress him, he needed a sling and hoist which was a hassle. When I had George on my run, I would take time to dress him, comb his hair and shave him, always talking to him whilst I went. He had a photo of a lady by his bed, and I would say "I guess this is your wife, George? She looks lovely" but he would never respond. I always felt much better having taken time and care to make all my residents look and feel their best. Putting them in pyjamas or joggers and a T-shirt was easier but they had many lovely clothes, and it was nice to make them feel good.

"Good morning, George" I said as I went in to wake him one morning. "Good morning," he replied. I jumped out my skin and ran up the hall to get the nurse to tell her that believe it or not George is speaking. She said that George doesn't speak and came with me to speak with him, he didn't respond, and so I thought that maybe I had imagined it. I got on with my work getting him ready on my own and put his shirt and tie on, pulled him up in the hoist and sat him in his wheelchair. I then gave him a wet shave and cleaned his glasses and brill creamed his hair, pushed him towards the mirror and said, "there you go George what a handsome man you are!". "Aww that's better," he said as he turned his head and made eye contact with me for the first time ever. "George, you can speak!" I said. George laughed and said, "yes I choose not to, and I hear much more, silence is sobering he said." He then told me I'd made him feel human again and went on to tell me he'd never forget that. I also discovered the lady in the photo was his daughter and that he was a fighter pilot in World War 2. He told me to look in his bottom drawer and I found a photo of a very good-looking pilot. "That's me, wasn't I handsome?" George wasn't the only one, many other residents had this strange awakening where they would talk to me and nobody else, and at the time I never really truly knew why. My understanding was kindness, they talk to me because I always treat them kindly, I would be asked to help give them medicine, take them to hospital etc. Kindness is everything. It changes people, situations, moments in time and can change the world. I truly believe it was my kindness that helped them open up.

It was then the end of my 4 days of working shift and I said goodbye and went home for my 3 days off. The night before I was due back at work, I woke in the middle of the night to the bedroom freezing cold. The whole house was cold. I got up to investigate and saw the bedroom window in my son's room wide open. I closed the window and went back to bed. Later I woke with the same cold breeze. This time I got up and went back to the room, and I saw George! There he was standing in his dressing gown and pyjamas in my son's room. "What the hell are you doing here?" I said. "I came to say thank you Steven" and he smiled and phased away. I was in shock. What happened? Was I hallucinating? Was I dreaming?
I got ready for work and made my way to work at 7am. I got to work for the handover and the charge nurse told us that George had passed away at 5am in his sleep. This was just 20 minutes after I'd seen him in my house. A warm feeling flooded through me, he was free from his body and back with his family. I went in to see his body as he lay in the same pyjamas and dressing gown that he had visited me in! I stroked his head and said thank you George. I could feel him behind me with that same reassuring smile he had before.

I believe that those of us closest to the spirit world and have a better ability to see are children and babies under 2 years old, and people close to their natural death, be it old age or something else. I'd like to add that if you start seeing spirit that doesn't mean you're about to kick the bucket, if you are reading this book, you probably have already been waking up for some time now and have a better awareness of the spirit world anyway.

Eddie was a loud man who had dementia, he would shout "Nurse, Nurse, help me, they are coming for me!" I'd always take some time to sit and chat with Eddie and much like many of the residents, he had lived a fantastic life and had many stories to tell. He was a small chap, just 5ft tall, and was bound to his wheelchair. His family would come see him twice a day and we had such a great connection. I went in to see Eddie who was in bed early every night just before the end of my shift and he said to me "they walk with you, you know?" I asked who, and Eddie responded, "the people of the light." Instinctively I knew he was seeing the spirit world around me. He said, "you see and feel them too." The morning after Eddie had said all of this to me, I woke up and felt a familiar uplifting presence. I went to work and started my routine of waking up my residents on my side of the hall. Eddie's room was last and usually I'd wake him up first because he made me laugh, but for some reason today I left him till last. I came out of one of the rooms with dirty bed sheets and saw Eddie standing by his door excited and full of life. "Eddie" I shouted, "be careful you will fall!", and as I ran to him, he ran back inside the room. "You, my friend, are going to end up falling and giving yourself a sore one." I said to his shape in the bed, his knees were up with the soles of his feet on the bed. "Eddie come on, up you get" I said, but when I got closer it was pretty clear that Eddie had actually passed away. He was cold to the touch so he had been gone for a wee while, but much like I could with my Grandad, I felt Eddie's bouncy energy still in the room. I knew that he just wanted me to know he was okay, and he was happy, and so that was the reason I saw him by his door that morning. He was checking in to let me know that he was all right.

Whilst doing my job at the care home, I had so many experiences that proved beyond reasonable doubt that the human soul does most certainly exist beyond physical death. As mediums, we are always seeking this truth, so it is so nice when we experience first-hand wonderful evidence. It was clear to me then that I needed to take the leap. I knew what I wanted to do with my mediumship skills and how to help others, and I was about to put everything on the line to create a wonderful place where evidence-based mediumship would be the life blood of everything we did.

For those who believe, no proof is necessary. For those who don't believe, no proof is possible.

Stuart Chase

Chapter 9
Spiritual churches and setting up my own

During all of my time working as a carer, I was still serving spiritualist churches and getting as much experience as a medium, and from this I'd like to give you some insight into the working life of a medium. It's lonely, often spending many hours travelling on your own across the country and turning up at community halls and churches not knowing anyone there. I would get bookings all across the country and was often given sat nav locations and I would drive to the location leaving plenty of time, so I was there on time. These car journeys are where I would converse with the spirit world, having wonderful conversations with them and asking for their help to allow me to work to the best of my ability. This was before cars had hands-free connections and I'm sure that many people must have looked at me thinking I'm mad! I would look in the rear-view mirror and talk hoping that they would think I had one of my kids in the back seat. I would sing the hymn, *Open My Eyes,* at the top of my voice and say "thank you, thank you" over and over to the spirit world for allowing me to work. Public demonstration work is usually about giving back to the community and the spirit world, and I would only ever take my fuel costs. I remember one time being so skint and serving a church in Glasgow, knowing that I could only go if I parked near a fuel station, so I had enough fuel for the journey home. In fact, I did like to park the car a short distance and walk to the church/centre I was demonstrating in because this always helped me to get a feel of the people in the local area and the local area itself. I still do it to this day. I love talking to people and by doing this I always feel connected to that community. Interestingly,

I would always get a free coffee or something kind would happen and that was always seen by me as a gift for my hard work. These would include seeing a white feather on the way to the church I was serving, hearing a particular song on the radio, or finding that I had a connection to the people running the church. Some of my closest friends would come from these centres and churches.

I realised in my time serving these churches that my own area really needed somewhere. I was often travelling to further afield places and wanted to bring something into the area I lived. It wasn't long before I knew the building I wanted to serve from, the local village hall, and so I started to make enquiries. Feathers were a theme, and I knew that the name had to resonate with my experiences over the years, so I chose to call the church Little Whispers Spiritual Centre, and I knew that the logo of the centre had to include a feather. In my true style, even though the venue wasn't confirmed, I took a leap of faith and went onto my social media to announce what was coming. I cannot tell you how amazing the response I had was, I was well known in the area for my work as a medium and this resulted in the community being excited to see this happening. I knew that spirit was assisting me as I met with the coordinator of the village hall, and it was confirmed that I'd be a keyholder and had the hall from every Monday with full use of the hall and facilities. I remember standing in the hall with keys in my hand and feeling a gathering of the spirit world! They were all around me. I could feel my family and many others surrounding me with pride! This was the right decision.

We had a venue, we had a keen interest and all we needed to do was book mediums. Through my work with spiritualist churches, I had gained a lot of medium friends who I could ask, and before long we had 26 weeks' worth of mediums booked to visit our church. This new church of mine drew people who wanted to help with the running of it, and before long I had help with the practical side of running the church - teas and coffees, looking after the congregation, building the community, marketing, and social media. Many special friendships were formed in this place, and it was a happy experience to be able to bring people together and make people feel cared for and healed in many ways, a true spiritual community. Following a lot of organisation and hard work preparing everything, it was finally time for opening night. We didn't know who to expect to walk through our doors and participate in the evening, but we knew it would be a success.

So, the time came to open the doors for the first night, and I stood at the door to greet people. Car after car filled the car park, cars filled with 4 or 5 people. We put out 25 chairs that night and 60 people came. We had to get more chairs and make plans for 60 seats each week, each empty chair in my mind was an invitation for someone. As the numbers grew, we had more people who came to help, and each chair was filled week after week. I realised that it was more than just the mediums drawing people in, it was also the sense of community and kindness that we had created. After that first night I got into my car full of adrenaline and a white feather sat perfectly in the passenger seat. This was a nod that I had created something very special. I sat with my heart full, looked up and said thank you. I can only imagine my energy as a glowing radiating beacon that day and everyone in contact with me must have felt it. White feathers were regular occurrences, and I would find out exactly who was delivering them very soon.

Human beings need connection and even without knowing it, we were growing an amazing community all powered by kindness. I didn't realise this at the time, I just thought we were doing a wonderful job and attracting many amazing people. The truth is that our power, our strength, was KINDNESS and the ability to make people feel valued and appreciated. Which is one of the fundamentals of being a medium - driving connection. Have you ever walked into a shop, and they know you by name? You feel a sense of belonging. I always make sure I get to know people's names and their stories. I also knew exactly how guest mediums were feeling so I was always able to facilitate this wonderful warm place and create a space that they felt as though they were coming home.

In this hall in the middle of Scotland, each week a medium would stand and deliver their mediumship for one hour. After which, we would hold a spiritual development circle to allow people the opportunity to explore their own spiritual connection. We ran the centre for 4 amazing years, delivering over 160 hours of mediumship as well as many outings, usually visiting haunted locations like Edinburgh underground vaults and raising money for charities. One of which was a local zoo's 'Save the Bears Fund', which was covered by the local press and national papers. We were creating a beautiful community that was a big part of my life. However, I had always kept my mediumship and my other working life really separate. Nobody at my other work knew what I did, I have no idea how I managed this, but I did. I'd been working my way up from a baker to a store manager in a national bakery chain. Things were about to level up on a massive scale both with the centre and with my working life and little did I know but my team at work had put the pieces together.

All our dreams can come true if we have the courage to pursue them.

Walt Disney

Chapter 10
Becoming 'The Soul Man'

One Monday morning I went to work as usual, opening the shop for 8am meant that I would start around 5:30am. I would check in the delivery, get the team organised and have the products out for opening. I loved my job, and I loved my team. My team worked hard for me because I was kind, and I ran one of the busiest, most profitable shops for the chain in Scotland. I was very proud. Even though I loved my team, I'd keep my personal life fairly private which is something my manager above me always advised. The team began coming into work and break times naturally started around 9am, I went for my break with a bacon roll and coffee, ready to start my admin for the day. There on my desk was a national Scottish newspaper, with a two-page spread reporting on a charity event we had done to raise funds for a local zoo. Around this time, the team began calling me '*The Soul Man*', what a daft name I thought! This wasn't the first time I had been called 'Soul Man', my friend who was a local hypnotherapist also called me the 'Soul Man' because of the work that I did. Seeing the article was really exciting, I was proud of what I had created and worked on, but admittedly I was also terrified of my team at work knowing about my separate spiritual work. Straight away I heard lots of comments from my team - "right Mr Soul Man give me a reading!" "I can't believe you never told us!" However, it became clear that nobody questioned my spiritual work and instead they were absolutely fascinated by it. Soon after my colleagues would start attending the centre, growing it even more. "Hello Mr Soul Man", people would start referring to me. Before long, the upper management got to know about my spiritual work and soon I was becoming really well known for that side of my work. As the months passed, I was asked more and more to do readings for people at work. Everything was fitting into place, and I didn't have to keep my spiritual life a secret anymore and what's more is that I was massively respected for my work.

I was attending my friend's class at a local spiritual shop when she asked me to do a platform demonstration for the class. I liked sitting in this class because they were spiritual people, it was a gathering and of course I'd learn some new things too. Even with years of experience under my belt, I knew then and still know now that I can learn from every environment and every experience. At that class I met a new friend who had such an infectious laugh, and I was drawn to her energy. We soon became really good friends with each other and also with another friend we met through this class. Over time, our connection grew, and I invited her to my spiritual centre, and she became more involved with the centre. Working with her, we made some small changes, and she became the vice president. During all of this time I was looking at a shop, I wanted to have a spiritual shop where I could sell some spiritual goods as well as do readings. The intention was always to keep the centre open as this belonged to the community, but I wanted to have a source of income from the work I loved the most. From the places available, I found premises that once belonged to a funeral director, and this seemed like the perfect place to be because of the type of work we were doing. With the success of the centre, it seemed natural to work with my new friend on this new business and we went into business together. My new shop, West Lothian's newest spiritual shop, was being born! This shop was a big learning step for me. I began to realise how I wanted to grow both as a medium and how I could help other people. Being at the shop soon became my main focus, and unfortunately, I took my eye off the centre. This was a hard lesson to learn. My team started to leave one by one and were replaced by others who then became workers at the shop. I was making mistakes because I was being blinded by my focus on the shop and I let people down who had helped me from the start. For that I will always be sorry. What I worked hard to create, was now being destroyed. These 4 years of running the spiritual centre taught me a very important lesson and led me to make one of the hardest decisions of my life and truly become The Soul Man.

Remember that everything that is happening around you, good or bad, is in some way conspiring to help you.

Latoya Alston

Finding the Medium Within You - 5

I speak often about how we live our lives determines who we are as mediums, and how we connect. Although people would think I was very successful, the truth was I was very unhappy and all because I wasn't being honest with myself. I had allowed myself to react instead of responding and I couldn't say how I felt. So, I believed that the spirit world had abandoned me in a way. I was looking for the answer to my problems to be something external when the whole time I was my problem. I had to find myself again and the best way of doing this was to do a deep dive into the superconscious, what was I missing. I sat one Friday evening feeling really sorry for myself and started to scan down my body and focus on my breath, the deeper I got the more connected I became. Soon I could feel them gathering, almost like they were being called to a meeting. The smell of leather and the tingles came, and suddenly I found myself in a waiting room with a large round table made of blue light. "Why has all of this happened?" I spoke out in my desperate pleas for help. I knew they were there, and a man appeared. I don't know who he was, but I knew he was safe. "Steven it's time for you to become what you have always meant to become, your true self, nobody to answer to. You have an important role here." Suddenly I was faced with a large pool of water and only my reflection. This was the point in which I connected with the essence of me. My own soul.

I'm going to ask you a question and I want you to answer as honestly as you can without thinking too much. Why are you here? Is it to work for 40 years, drive a nice car, make money, have kids, and then retire only to die maybe 20 years or more if you're lucky? Why are you here?

Take the time to meditate, to quieten down all the noise, all the chaos. This will take practice and patience.

For myself, I knew that the question the water was asking me was just this. Why was I here? I knew the answer was I am here to help as many people as I can. However, my purpose for being here is also way more than that, my friend. My purpose here is to change people's thinking, it's to challenge the normal ways of thinking and inspire people to become the best versions of themselves. My purpose is to be of the highest service to other people.

Self-care is not self-indulgence, it is self-preservation.

Audre Lorde
Feminist and civil rights leader

Chapter 11
When Angels intervene

Remember the feathers all around me that I kept seeing? I was about to understand who was delivering the feathers and up to this point I still had every faith that it was the spirit world giving confirmation that I was on the right path. My wife is Irish catholic and has a wonderful faith in her God. I love that she has so much faith and all of our children have been brought up Catholic with my spiritual twist. I really truly believe that faith is important for everyone, not necessarily religion, as religion was created by the human race and is only an interpretation of many minds.

I love to sit in a chapel. It's a wonderful and peaceful energy. Churches are spiritual power houses that house amazing people from every walk of life. Father George was a wonderful new age priest, I knew instinctively he had sight like mine, he was able to see and sense the spirit world and the presence of the divine. Father George was 5ft 11, thick glasses, and a blonde mullet hairstyle on top of his slim body. He was always so full of energy. He was southern Irish and spoke as fast as he moved, his faith in the divine was unwavering although he understood the love of all faiths. Even in the work I did, he said there was great good, and God's love passed my lips with the healing work it did. Father George just knew things and when he lay his hands on your shoulder you could feel a hot energy blasting from his fingertips. It is my belief that the higher power, call it God, the universe, or the universal life force, it works through kind people, people pure of heart to administer healing. Kindness is the life blood of being a medium. When Father George laid his hands on your shoulder an instant calm would come across you, his words sang with warm peaceful tones. He was very healing, and I would struggle to find any fault in him. Even when my wife and I told him we were being married in the spiritualist church he said, "how fine it is to marry in such a place of love."

I was about to see an Angel for the first time channelled through Father George. We attended a mass for the sick at the church one evening, the church was a small community church that from the outside looked like a derelict building. However, when you walked through the doors you were greeted with the same sweet smell of incense, holy water font to bless yourself, and the grand hall with pews on either side with a grand altar at the front. Father George stood at the base of the altar dressed in a long white robe, the sun beamed through the stained-glass windows giving the whole space a feeling of complete peace, he started his sermon talking about healing and I just zoned out as I always do at church. People then started to queue for their blessing where Father George would anoint each person with a holy oil. As he was anointing, I was instantly aware of giant hands on his shoulders and a man around 7ft tall. This apparition had blonde mullet hair style and looked perfect in every way. Above his shoulders, a white haze in the shape of wings but not the fluffy white feathers you normally associate with Angels. My eyes trembled and my body froze in shock. This ethereal being smiled as each person stepped forward with a burst of bright energy moving from his shoulders down through his hands and channelled down into Father George's hands. I turned to my wife and mother-in-law in awe telling them what I was seeing, they both looked at me with a very confused look. The Angel then turned his head and made eye contact with me, I instantly had a warm feeling move through my whole being. In that moment, an instant feeling of Deja vu. I have experienced this feeling before.

After the service there was tea and biscuits served, and Father George made his way around the room chatting with everyone who had attended the mass. I wondered if he was aware of what I had seen. I had a good enough relationship with him to ask and so said

"Father George, were you aware of what was happening behind you in there?" I made sure not to mention the Angel, especially as my mother-in-law laughed nervously. "The Angel you mean?" He replied confidently before he winked and moved on to the next table. Nicky and her mum were gobsmacked that he had felt what I had seen. This was an extraordinary experience, and I believe that when Angels choose to show themselves to you there will be many more experiences. They usually are not one-off experiences! Why? Because we are now attuned to their energy.

This moment with Father George enabled me to understand a moment in my life. I now understood who the mystery men were that appeared to me many years earlier. A few years before I set up the centre and around the time I met my wife, I was a young 19-year-old excited about going to the pub with my friends from work. We were going to a local pub in Fountainbridge in Edinburgh and walking across as a large group, chatting away like you do at that age. We were crossing a really busy road with an island in the middle when all of my friends crossed the road and I got stuck in the middle of the road. Then suddenly I was aware of two tall men with dark sunglasses on in dark suits, they looked like two men in black agents standing either side of me and were about 6 ft 4 inches. The interesting thing is that I don't remember how they got there. When they appeared, it was almost like time stopped still. The cars were still passing by however there was this eerie sense of silence almost like I was standing in a bubble. One of the men put his hand on my shoulder and he said, "hello Steven". I looked up at him and said "who are you? How do you know my name?" He looked down at me and said, "that doesn't matter Steven, what matters is we are here with you now." I looked to the other side of me where the other tall man stood, as it was pretty clear that they were together. I instinctively looked down my uniform to see if I was wearing my name badge, "seriously, how do I know you?" The first one said, "you are going to do some amazing work for us, you are going to help many people". Now at this point in time I thought that these two men were mystery shoppers from my work, I said "are you from my work?" They said "no but we do help you and we will continue to help you, even when things feel tough, know that we are always with you, always. Helping you, always supporting you, never forget Steven, you were put here for a reason."

At that moment as quickly as they had come, they disappeared. I felt a huge gush of wind and they were gone. At the time I worked alongside my best friend. We had been friends for many years, since we were very small. I said to him when I arrived at the pub, "did you see those two guys standing with me on the island?" He replied "what two guys? You were just standing there staring." I know that these two men were Angels. I felt it in my gut and the same feeling came as I saw the Angel at the church, I felt love and care. Even though I didn't know who they were, I felt safe, secure, and looked after by these perfect strangers. I believe Angels work with the human race in human form a lot to help and inspire people at their highs and lows.

Have you ever been in a situation where you have felt so desperate, and this wonderful feeling of calm comes across you for no apparent reason? I believe this is the Angels working with us to let us know everything is going to be okay. When I'm in a situation where I feel like the world is crashing around me, I'm always reminded of their presence by a random white feather showing up or combinations of numbers like 1111 being thrown into my awareness. I always say thank you for the reminder and things get better. Even while writing this sentence, I look at my phone and the time is 22:22.

Calling upon the Angels when we are in need, helps the Angels fulfil their heavenly mission. We are truly co-creators with them.

Aileen Anglin

Chapter 12
Starting Again

Here is the point in which my whole life was about to take the biggest U-turn with the birth of my amazing business, The Soul Man and Friends - Scotland's Spiritual Hub. I had left my previous business and was working as a self-employed manager for a large UK weight loss organisation which helped people feel good, lose weight, and change their lives. Another incarnation of me trying to help as many people as I could to be the best version of themselves. I loved my role, however I couldn't do this from home, so I decided to hire a small office in the local business centre. The office was about 10 square ft and was situated in the old doctor surgery in West Calder, West Lothian, just a stone's throw away from my previous business. The building had an intercom system, and my office was to the right of the entry door down the end of a long corridor. I had a desk, a fridge, a sink, and a large worktop on the back wall against windows that stretched across the whole room. I worked so hard and put everything I could into my work, but I missed the spiritual environment greatly. No matter how I decorated my office it just felt cold. So, I started to add spiritual items like buddhas, Angels and my Tarot cards. Finally, this felt like a space that felt more like home, but I found myself being distracted and more and more drawn to my tarot, asking questions like "is this the right job for me?" and surely enough the cards always gave me the answer that I should be of service helping people.

I was frustrated and felt my attention slipping every day. I wanted to work with the spirit world but that wouldn't pay my bills so I would give myself a talking to every single week convincing myself that this was the right thing to do. But what happens when we ignore what our subconscious is telling us? It only gets worse. It's like a jar of bees with no lid, in order to keep the bees in you have to use your hand to cover the jar, the bees will sting but soon get used to you and calm down, then you starve the bees of oxygen, and they die. This is like your hopes and dreams, my room was full of bees because I couldn't keep my hand on the jar. I was ignoring what was happening all around me.

One Monday morning my buzzer went off in the office which was so unusual. Who was buzzing me? Someone must have the wrong unit. "Hello" I said, the voice on the other end replied, "hello is this Steven?" "Hi yes, it's Steven, how can I help you?" I am here for a reading? Are you able to fit me in?" At that moment I knew intuitively that this person had been sent to see me for a reason, so I cleared my desk and said, "yes come along I'll meet you at the door." I didn't know what type of reading I was doing so I just went along with it. I opened the door to see a really vulnerable looking smaller lady. "Hello honey how are you, would you like a cup of tea or coffee?" The offer of tea was a simple gesture but was also a kind thing to do, it immediately put her at ease. As I made her tea the smell of old leather and mould filled the air, my skin tingled, and that familiar feeling of joy consumed me. This was my work this was where I was happiest. Helping people to heal from the passing of a loved one, I knew that this work today was going to help this lovely lady in so many ways. I could feel a man's energy which to me felt like her husband, a proud man who didn't really understand how mediumship worked in life and was perhaps a little dismissive of the work of a medium. I knew I had my work cut out for me however I just embraced the process knowing that she needed this.

We will call her Sylvia for the purpose of the book. "Okay Sylvia let me explain how I connect, my job today is to connect with the spirit world and prove to you beyond reasonable doubt that your loved ones are still around you. Today's reading isn't necessarily about your life, it's simply to give you proof. I do this by closing my eyes and asking your loved ones to work with me. It's important for me that you just say yes or no, the less I know the better because my mind will fill in the gaps or make assumptions. Do I have your permission to work with your loved ones and confirmation that you will just say yes or no?" "Yes absolutely," she said. "What's also important Sylvia is that I may not make a connection today, but we will establish that quite quickly. In this instance it's important that we stop the reading because if there's no evidence then we can't continue. This doesn't mean anything is wrong, it's just maybe not the right day. And lastly, it's important that what your loved ones share with you should never impact your life in a way that it encourages you to go away and make life altering decisions like sell your home or anything else. I know if my great grandmother told me to go sell my house I certainly wouldn't go away and sell because my dead granny told me so" I laughed as I added this light touch and asked, "does all of this make sense Sylvia?"

"Yes, absolutely Steven" I had set up her expectations for the reading and was ready to go. This is something that's so important in the role of a medium, framing up what to expect and making it really clear what both your role is in the reading. In the past I remember sitting with people who would say "hello what's your name? Okay let's get started". The whole process would be a bit all over the place. But when you frame up properly, it's like setting up your plans for a business meeting. Everyone knows what to expect including the spirit world. I will speak about this more in the next mediumship training section. Let's get back to Sylvia. So, I closed my eyes and connected with the familiar tingles and old leather and instantly felt the same man's energy behind me, "has your husband passed Sylvia?", "yes, he has" she confirmed. Then she got really upset and said, "can you give me his name?" A question I get asked so many times, like I mentioned before relying on only sight to know somethings there is pretty silly and so is relying on a medium to get a name, In Scotland everyone can take a Margaret, Betty, John, Jimmy, so of course mediums will hit the nail on the head eventually, however can they describe in great detail and accuracy the detail of the passing, the look, the personality? That's the power of great evidence, you don't need a name if you can provide all the rest. Now I would love to name every person I connect with but that's not a pressure I need, I don't know why it doesn't work that way, but it doesn't. "Let's just focus on getting the rest right Sylvia, he shows me that he had a problem in the left ventricle of the heart, does that make sense? Yes, okay although this isn't what took him over, but his heart had a weakness. He shows me an infection in his lungs, and I believe this was what made him desperately unwell and took him over, is that correct?" "Yes, it is," she said. It's so important that a medium checks understanding throughout in order to know that the information is correct, otherwise what's the point? We need constant validation to keep our connection strong. During the validation process she also got very upset, which is the part of my job I hate as I don't want to upset people, so it's vital we give time and space to allow processing. We must also keep checking in with our sitter's emotional wellbeing, that it is okay to continue, if they want to take a breather etc.

We got to the end of the communication and Sylvia let out this huge sigh of relief. She had no doubt in her mind that her husband was okay, but she was worried because of his strong belief that the afterlife was a load of nonsense that he would go somewhere else. One thing that every single communicator always wants to pass on to me to share with them is that they are okay, they always say "please tell them that I'm okay". It's always loaded with emotion, I feel that emotion as I write these words, feeling the echoes of the thousands of souls I've helped over the years. When I work with spirit, I can feel many things, and I'd like to share with you the feeling that I get once I've finished working with someone. First of all, behind me from the spirit world comes this wave of peace, you know at a concert when the song everyone loves comes on and the crowd ripples with excitement, that's what hits me, a blow of emotional peace and joy, then the peace that the sitter feels. They keep thanking me and I'm just so grateful that I was able to provide proof. It's such a massive responsibility to have someone that the person loves so very much and get every part of information correct. My heart feels full knowing that I have helped two people and sometimes whole families heal.

After Sylvia they just kept coming, my buzzer would go sometimes four or five times a day with people looking for readings. I had to block off a whole day in my diary to accommodate the amount of people wanting readings and I had a waiting list of people happy to wait months in advance. Then one night just before I was about to leave 5 people turned up for a meditation class that I had not organised! I still don't know to this day how or why they turned up, but I figured if they are here then there's a reason for it. It started to become a real stretch, my friends called me 'Soul Man' because of the work I do, and they would send their friends and colleagues, as well as family members, for readings with me. Before long, the buzzer would go with people asking if I was the Soul Man. I sat at my desk one day with the window open, working away on the laptop in my day job and outside at the community centre across the road a car was playing the song "I'm a Soul Man" by Sam and Dave. I sat and chuckled to myself, it's a sign! "Come on then" I said to the invisible army, "what do you want me to do?" I didn't know at the time I was about to step into the role of The Soul Man in a big way.

That day driving home I felt a compulsion to stop the car next to a public park I drove past every evening, I got out of the car and looked at the setting sun. It was January and the busiest time for the weight loss organisation, so I was being well paid, but instantly it all came hurtling at me in an overwhelming way. THE SOUL MAN. And my friends, I would open my own shop with a very different vibe and the team to help me would be my friends, no staff just helpful people. And that shop would be in Broxburn West Lothian, don't ask me how or why Broxburn but Broxburn it had to be! A thrill and excitement came over me in that moment and I knew that's what all of this was preparing me for! So, it was time to go home and tell my lovely Nicky. I sat back in the car and there came another sign, this time in the lyrics of the song from the Greatest Showman musical which played on the radio in perfect sync with my epiphany - *From Now On*. The song resonated in so many ways, but the main points were:

- In all that pain there was so much learning

- All that pain led me back to working with Spirit
- I would never let anyone else bind my vision and would do it my way
- I can't wait till tomorrow I need to act now

That promise I made to the spirit world all those years ago was about to be reborn into a very different spiritual space that would be inclusive to everyone. Treating everyone with fairness, kindness and providing space for people to feel safe and looked after. So, with the events of that day, The Soul Man Limited was born, the first incarnation of what you see today.

Often it's the deepest pain which empowers you to grow into your highest self.

Karen Salmansohn

Finding the Medium Within You - 6

When you are conducting a mediumship reading it's so important to frame up how you are going to conduct the reading, and your responsibility. Did you see how I did this by explaining to Sylvia exactly what the process would involve? A reading should always be a really positive experience for people, with a clear understanding of the whole process. Often people come to see a medium when they are grieving and are particularly vulnerable, so it's vital that the utmost care is given and that you are honest if you aren't making a connection.

I have spoken about this before, but the role of a medium is such a massive responsibility. We are counsellors in many ways, we are caregivers when people are highly vulnerable and emotional. We must look after them properly. Think how damaging it could be to do a reading for someone not knowing how they were afterwards, not knowing what the effect of your words have had? I believe that every person working in my field should have at least some basic knowledge of mental health first aid or have done some sort of counselling or coaching work. The reason being is that some people genuinely just need something more, some people don't need a reading, they need help and support in other areas. If you are able to signpost, that's looking after people, that's genuinely caring. I would feel absolutely awful if I hadn't noticed that someone needed more than a reading. I have done many different courses over the years on coaching, counselling, and lately mental health first aid. Why? Because it means I can help people on a whole other level by signposting and providing a service of care and compassion. Believe it or not I have kindly refused to read someone on multiple occasions because they haven't been in a good place, and I've been able to get them much needed help and support.

It's also important to mention in this section that I have also been unable to read many people over the years for various reasons. It is rare but it does happen, and a lot of people will ask why. The reason is I may not be the right person for that person in the spirit world. Now, I'm a warm and caring person who pretty much gets on with everyone I meet with the exception of a few. Those few I meet in life that I don't connect with aren't bad people, it's just that I don't vibe with them for whatever reason, it's exactly the same in the spirit world. I am never going to connect with someone I don't vibe with. I've heard many different theories on the levels that exist in the spirit world, planes of existence where good and bad move up and down the levels. However, in my experience we all exist on the same plane just like we do on earth, but much like here we avoid certain people we wouldn't connect with. For example, you wouldn't find a high court judge in the spirit world mixing in the same circles as murderers, would you? So, when I have someone in the spirit world connecting with me who wasn't a very nice character in life, the chances of me making an established positive connection with them are pretty slim. Also, if the sitter themselves is not warm friendly and they come across judgmental, it's so difficult for me to make a good connection with them and so the reading for me would have to stop.

This is a vital skill of working with people with bodies and without. To be able to say no and to stop yourself being completely drained by someone's energy.

Make some notes on this section.

- Why do you think it's so important for the medium to work responsibly?
- Have you ever had a reading that felt uncomfortable or unprofessional?
- Do you see readings differently now after this section?

If you realise your responsibility you will realise your destiny.

Tasneem Hameed

Chapter 13
Finding a shop

The vision was clear of what I needed to do and all I needed was a shop to operate from and I knew as I said before that Broxburn was the location, so I started searching the internet for shops to let. I asked my good friend to come with me to view a shop which was previously a Chinese restaurant. We drove to Broxburn and parked in the large car park on Greendykes Road. Walking up the road towards the traffic lights I looked across to see a bright yellow shop named the Polish Food Shop. I liked the look of it and the energy it vibrated, but it appeared occupied, so we kept walking and walked up to the old Chinese restaurant. The unit was large and stripped right back to the stone walls, I couldn't see a way it could work and very quickly I could feel the disappointment. I said to myself this isn't right, I could also feel the invisible armies nudge that this wasn't the right space. Back to the drawing board! I had this unwavering belief that we would find the right space.

We walked along the main street looking for available shops but there was nothing, so we walked up the main street to the local bakers to get a coffee and a cake, and standing in the doorway my phone pinged. My friend who I had not seen for some time had messaged me via Facebook Messenger to ask me what I was doing in Broxburn. I looked around me and couldn't see her, and she messaged that she was working in the estate agent premises right across the street. I waved across the road and replied that we had been looking at a shop but it wasn't right. I was gutted. She told me that they had a couple of retail units on their books and could send me the details. I gave her my email address and by the time my coffee was ready I had an email in my inbox with only one shop. To my absolute amazement it was the yellow Polish Food Shop, and it was vacant! I couldn't believe my eyes. She offered to take me round to look at it, so after grabbing my coffee and blurting out to my friend what had happened and she replied, "oh my god Miagi (her nickname for me) it's a sign!" I looked up in the middle of the street and said to the invisible army "if this is it, I need you to give me some sort of sign!"

I counted the steps and could feel my excitement building…*thirty-five, thirty-six*. The smell of leather and mould was around, I knew they were building all around me, like an invisible conga line as my skin tingles all over my body. *Seventy-eight, seventy-nine* "oh Miagi can you feel them" my friend said. *One hundred and ten, one hundred and eleven* we were there one hundred and eleven steps. The shop had large shutters controlled by a keyhole on the wall, my friend from the estate agent turned the key and the mechanical electric shutters started moving up, my body tingling like mad with so much excitement and in we stepped. I couldn't believe my eyes.

A single moment in time can change your whole life forever and this was one of those moments, the shop was tiny, about the same size as my office, it was jam packed with people from my invisible army, what an overwhelming feeling of love now occupied the space. "Steven, look," said my friend. We looked down at the floor and a Halloween decoration, glow in the dark ghost with the wavy tail, sat on the floor next to a white feather and a tea bag. This was the sign I was looking for, "thank you, thank you" I said out loud to my invisible spectators. Of all the things to see, this certainly was a sign considering the main part of the shop I wanted to be tea leaf reading and mediumship. The white feather confirmed also that this was the right place! There was a small bathroom and an old derelict storage room to the back of the shop, but it was so very small, how on earth would we fit tables and chairs in this space to turn it into a spiritual hub, we will make this work, "I'll take it" I said without hesitation, so we went along to the estate agents and signed all the paperwork. The only thing we had to wait for was our landlord to sign the lease and give us our agreement!

Seventeen days of waiting for that confirmation was the longest seventeen days of my life. I checked my phone for emails or text messages every single day until the seventeenth day when they called me to say that everything was ready, and I could come to collect the keys. I wanted to get them straight away but due to it being so late in the day, I had to wait until the morning. That night felt like Christmas Eve, I couldn't hold my excitement any longer. I needed to tell people, so I went to the field that I went to for guidance. It was covered with dandelion wish flowers all over the grass. It was such a magical scene. I logged into my Facebook account and typed in the title West Lothian's newest spiritual shop to a live feed and once I saw the icon go live, I clicked that go live button. *Three two one, you are now live*! To everyone I knew on Facebook I said: "Hi everyone, I have some really exciting news, in a couple of month's time I will be opening West Lothian's newest spiritual shop! I get the keys tomorrow and I will share more in time!" There were so many people commenting and saying how excited they were that I was back! Three hundred people watched that live broadcast and liked our page, in 24 hours we had one thousand two hundred new page likes, it was going crazy and really well received.

That night I tossed and turned wondering if I was doing the right thing. What if my old business thought I was trying to steal their custom, and what if it didn't work out? But also, lots of really exciting thoughts, like how would it look? How would I bring it all together and what would we do? There was so much to think about. The next day I woke up with the most amazing feeling. I was so excited, I danced around the house with my wife and kids. My appointment was at 10am and so I got into the car and took some deep breaths. Quite often for myself, as I drive I speak to the spirit world. I'm sure people think I'm on the phone but usually I'm conversing with the invisible army. I sat in the car that morning and asked them to give me another sign to let me know that this is the place before I signed the lease. Then on cue the radio in the car played *From Now On* from The Greatest Showman! It was another sign I was doing the right thing. So, I went to get the keys and signed the lease. I had them in my hand and the first thing on my agenda was to go and sit in the shop on my own. I walked round the corner and put my key in the shutter for the first time, as the shutters moved up the excitement was overwhelming. I then put my key in the door, I was home. I sat in the shop looking at the space which was much smaller than I remembered and had this overwhelming feeling, what have I done? I had no furniture, no tea making facility and a back room that needed a joiner and a plumber. I had a limited amount in my savings and that would have to cover it! My Granny had offered me a loan already to pay the deposit and buy some furniture, but a friend stepped in and loaned me the money instead, and for that I will always be grateful. This touches on the Law of Attraction, when we are putting out there to the universe that we need help then we must accept when we have that offer of help. I was so reluctant to accept help, but I did because otherwise how would I be able to do all I needed to do!

That evening I got my wife and kids and took them down to the shop and every one of them said "oh it's really small, isn't it?" I told them that I will make this work, to start small and think big. Then I went to collect my friend who came to view the shop. We went inside and she said "oh Miagi, it's smaller than I remember". This time I had taken a kettle, two cups, and cleaning supplies. We sat on two-fold out chairs staring at each other and then staring at the shop. Both of us couldn't believe what was happening. Then the emotions hit me, I couldn't control myself and got really upset, good tears and I guess, overwhelm. We had the bare bones of a shop, a new business incorporated but I was about to realise the many obstacles that were about to make the dream come true even harder to get off the ground.

It's not enough to be in the right place at the right time. You have to be the right person in the right place at the right time.

T. Harv Eker

Chapter 14
Juggling

Everything was grinding to a halt with the planning of the shop because I still had to work full time and earn a wage to support my family. This was the hardest part because all I wanted to do was be there full time, but for now I had to juggle. Opening a business may look easy, you just have to find a premises and make your dream work. As long as you stay determined and focussed on your dream then you can make it work, and the reality is many sleepless nights and lots of changing the plans to suit the current situation. I was very aware of how I wanted things to look, and I knew that they would get to that point but for now that wasn't to be, we had to work with what we had. The most important thing was we had to have the shop usable and ready to open and in order to do this we needed the building works done in the back shop.

I sat in the shop in my chair looking around me for support from the spirit world and said out loud, "I need your help again guys, I need someone to help me, please send me someone who can make all this happen". I was at my Mum's later that night telling her everything I needed to do and my uncle who was there at the time said, "let me make a few calls, Steven, and I'll get back to you with a plan on how I might be able to help". On my way home that evening as I was driving my uncle called me, "Steven can you meet me at the shop?" he asked. So, I drove to the shop and waited for my uncle to come. His friend had a look at what needed to be done and how he could help. I explained what he needed, and he replied that he could do all that and asked me my budget. I knew that my budget was small, but he was sure he could make it work. 24 hours later he had the keys and started work. They both worked into the early hours and after 2 days I got a phone call to let me know that it was all done and to come have a look. Driving to the shop felt like Christmas again, I was so excited to see what they had done. I got to the shop and couldn't believe my eyes. Not only had they done an amazing job, but they had also installed a hot water boiler, a new LED window in the back restoring an old feature window, and also, they had created a window seat made with resin. There was a dragonfly pendant light fitting in the front shop area creating a new seating area we could be proud of. All of this was possible with my uncle's friend's joinery, electrical and plumbing skills, "why did you do all this?" I asked. "Because I feel a massive urge to want to help you, Steven. I'm blown away by your kindness." I told him how grateful I was and asked how I could ever repay him. He said, "your uncle tells me how you do so much for others and ask for nothing in return, all I ask is you keep doing that amazing work."

I've spoken previously about kindness and how it can move mountains and how our invisible reputation is seen by many more people than we can know. What was happening now was a direct result of that vibration of kindness, call it the universe, God, a higher power or my invisible army, someone somewhere was helping in ways I couldn't explain. When we are kind and compassionate and do good things, everything around us responds in the same way. I was energetically attracting the right people to help me create my dream. I spent the next couple of days finishing the decoration and now it was time to announce our opening day. We had a shop, it was finished and ready for opening. We needed signage above the shop but for now it was important to get the shop open. I had my people ready to go, the same way I had attracted people to help get the shop ready, I had also attracted the right team. Weeks before we opened I met with one of my friends at my office in West Calder telling her my plans to open. She was so excited to be part of the new team and helped me decorate along with my other two friends. So, I had three helpful people who made up The Soul Man and Friends first team. A tribe of people would help create this amazing new business, but I still had to work full time, so I needed a fourth person and again the universe delivered another friend to help, and the team was complete. The evening before the opening day came, there was such a buzz with the team, we all worked together late into the night cleaning and getting ready for opening. The shop was ready and as we stood outside looking in at our hard work, my heart burst with gratitude! An overwhelming feeling of astonishment that we had been able to get to this point after so many problems. That evening I went home and couldn't sleep yet again. Everything I had worked so hard to achieve was happening all in a whirlwind 6-month period.

On the morning of opening, I got up early and sat on my back doorstep at home, looked up and said thank you for making this happen. I was inspired at that point to go to the shop and buy a huge bunch of flowers for our first customer, so I kissed my wife and kids goodbye. Nicky said, "good luck darling, I'm so proud of you!" And off I went into the day with the best feeling I have ever felt. From now on I will do this right, from now on I will create a warm friendly community. Admittedly, all the time in the back of my mind I couldn't help but think about my full-time job and how the demands of working 2 full time jobs would be so difficult, however, I marched on thinking it would all be okay. I trusted that no matter what I was doing the right thing with The Soul Man and Friends, and even though people around me would be thinking that I couldn't do both, I had this unwavering belief that everything would work out the way it was meant to. I was about to learn what I already knew that people and community are essential in running a business, but also the hard lesson that in order to be the best you can be you must prioritise your time effectively and not overdo it working two jobs. This hard lesson was just around the corner.

I believe that everything happens for a reason. People change so that you can learn to let go. Things go wrong so that you can appreciate them when they're right, you believe lies so you'll eventually learn to trust no one but yourself. And sometimes good things fall apart so better things can fall together.

Marilyn Monroe

Chapter 15
Tough times

Opening day was amazing. Our first customers were delighted with their flowers and before we knew it the first week was done! The shop was buzzing and busy every single day. What I didn't realise was that the shop would begin to pull people together and drive connections between people. The design of the shop was small and while people were in the shop, they would have no option but to speak to each other. The one thing I was worried about was the one thing that had the opposite effect. People were talking and forming new relationships, this was exactly what I wanted but instead of trying to make it happen it happened by default. As word got out more and more people started talking about us and how they felt like friends once they left, this was down to our amazing team and myself who were always so warm and friendly. Our new motto was born and would be the cornerstone of everything we do, "Come in a stranger, return as a friend". You'll see this message on my door to this day.

We then started to have people ask us if we would do classes and workshops, which would come to be the first incarnation of the Soul Man Academy, and so with ease we started classes every Sunday and Thursday on my nights off. I was working 40 hours at my job and 35 hours at the shop but loving every minute, I was busy and that kept me operating at a high level. We then began workshops on Sundays also covering subjects such as Tea Leaf reading, Law of Attraction, and many other things, but essentially my goal was all about helping people to develop themselves first. We also started a meditation class just for men initially and then a mixed class, the meditation for men attracted some positive press coverage in a national Scottish newspaper. There was so much going on and my time was becoming more and more scarce. I was spinning many plates and expecting my team at the shop to do everything whilst I wasn't present enough at the shop. It was growing in many areas, but the team needed me there and as a result people began to get unhappy with the workload. Then I made the decision to employ three more people without even thinking about the implications, simply because I was trying to fire-fight and take the pressure off. Now I've swithered about whether to put this into the book simply because it could be perceived as a negative but it's an important part of the journey! I now had seven people to pay, and I wasn't there to monitor how things were. At Christmas time in 2018, a week before Christmas, I simply didn't have any money in the business bank account to pay the extra three wages. I panicked. I had taken my foot off the gas, so I had to fund the wage bill from my own wage from my full-time job to compensate. I was starting to drop the plates I was spinning, and everything felt as though I was spinning in the dark blindfolded. I knew that the only thing to do was leave my full-time job, but instead I carried on pledging more of my time to the shop. However, instead of things getting better, the focus was slipping from my full-time job. I loved my job, but I loved my business more. I could catch up on my work. I was a focussed hard-working guy, and I would fix the stuff I hadn't done at my work. I carried on stuffing all of my focus to The Soul Man and Friends, and telling my boss that I would catch up, that I was just busy with my other job.

The Soul Man and Friends was the best place for people to be and my loyalty lay there, I could help people, my team loved having me there and sure enough what you focus on grows. Things started to change from this point, with some of the team members moving on for the right reasons. I was learning that in order for the shop to work, I needed to be around even more. The shop got busier, and we were absolutely buzzing with positive energy, every day going to work was a pleasure. Then the emails would come from my boss at the weight loss organisation that were highlighted in bright yellow capitals with the text 'Right team, I need this done by Monday'. So,

I would do what was asked of me, all whilst reading at the shop and working late nights until I was done. I was stressed and I started to eat junk food. Before I knew it, I was gaining weight and feeling depressed all whilst trying to maintain some balance. My marriage became strained, and the kids would complain I was grumpy and didn't have time for them. When I was at The Soul Man and Friends, I was living my happiest life, but it was so wrong, everything was out of balance. I wasn't seeing friends, my family and becoming more and more isolated by my focus on work. I looked up and asked my invisible army, "please help me to sort this out folks, I can't maintain this anymore." My prayer was about to be answered but not in the way I expected, which would change everything in the most devastating way.

In the middle of September 2019 everything fell apart. This was one of the most life changing days of my life and I certainly didn't see it coming. I was going to a 1-to-1 with my boss at the weight loss organisation and I was really excited about this as my boss had known I was struggling and not getting things done. She had said to do the minimum until my next 1-to-1, and we would create a plan. The meeting was held, as always, at a local hotel. When I entered, she gave me a hug as usual and asked if I wanted a coffee, but something felt off. Her line manager was there too, a lady I really loved as she was so inspiring in how she worked. I looked up to her in many ways and wished she were my line manager. The coffee arrived and my boss asked me to explain why I hadn't done certain tasks. I looked at her confused as I was very aware that she knew all about everything I wasn't managing. To this day I question if she knew, or I had just dreamed up our conversations. I am not someone who tells lies and has always told the truth. The truth always sets us free no matter what. So, I explained that I was aware that I hadn't done my job and for that I was very sorry. I offered to do whatever it took to fix it. I was aware of unseen energy between her and her boss and this felt like an ambush. Something was wrong, I didn't want to get her into trouble so I just spoke the truth hoping she would agree and put in a plan to fix things. Then she said, "Steven I have no option but to let you go, I can't trust you" and she started to get upset. My insides turned upside down, my heart thumped in my chest and a lump in my throat appeared. My lip started to tremble, and I started to cry uncontrollably. It was 11 weeks till Christmas. I needed my full-time wage, and she was sacking me. "What does that mean?" I asked, confused in the moment. "It means I am removing your manager role Steven, we don't want to lose you completely. You are good at your job, but the manager role isn't right for you." I couldn't argue as I hadn't done my job correctly and I expected to have had some sort of structure or procedure to support me to do better, but instead I was discarded. I am not proud of how I acted and kept asking them to reconsider as I sobbed for about 30 minutes.

I stepped out of that room that day with utter devastation. I had to explain to my wife that I had been sacked for the first time in my life. I felt like a failure, I am such a proud person and couldn't see past my grief. I sat in the car and messaged our manager's group chat to tell them what had happened, and they were all shaken and in disbelief as they were also aware that if they weren't managing things then we would get help and support to fix it. After some lovely supportive messages, I felt good enough to drive home, the closer I got to home the more the dread sunk in. How could I tell Nicky what had just happened? How would she even understand as I hadn't spoken about how I was struggling. As I drove home, I kept driving and I found myself at South Queensferry getting close to the sea to find some balance. I parked in the car park by the Forth Road Bridge and began walking to the middle of the bridge, the wind was refreshing, walking against the hard cold wind was cathartic. I found myself in the centre of the bridge so upset and so very low, looking at my phone for a missed call from my boss or a text to check how I was after being so visibly distraught in the hotel, but there was nothing from anyone. At that moment I felt so intensely low that I stepped up onto the fence of the bridge. What am I doing? I thought to myself. I've so much to live for. But the urge to jump and end this acute pain felt so overwhelming. I was one decision away from potentially ending my life, I knew what was waiting for me if I did jump and that my wife and kids would be okay without me. I was rationalising all of my thinking and making it okay to do this. How long would it take? Would it be painful? What if I hit a rock? What if a child found me on the beach? All this because someone treated me badly and behaved in a way that hurt me so deeply that everyone else in my life would be without me. I believe completing suicide is one the hardest decisions anyone can make. I remember a story I had read about people who had jumped from the Golden Gate Bridge, San Francisco, USA, and the discussion about how the minute their hands left the railing they had instant regret.

In that moment as I stood there trying desperately to rationalise everything, I was reviewing my life, everything flashing before my eyes, the wind pushing against my back almost as if it were urging me to jump, was this a sign. This time I wasn't asking my invisible army for help, I've never felt so alone and so helpless. Suddenly, in that moment of helplessness I felt a sudden urge of adrenaline and I stepped forward again holding the freezing railings and reliving the pain of the evening, when clear as a bell I heard "Steven you have more to do, we have cleared your path." At that moment I took a breath, suddenly I was aware of the smell of leather and my skin was tingling. They were all around, supporting me and willing me to live, like magic the wind stopped as did time itself. I have more to give, of course I do, I can fully immerse myself in work. I asked them for a way forward and they have helped facilitate this. I took a penny out of my pocket and looked at it, mentally pushing all that emotion that filled up inside me into the penny, and then I threw it with all of my might ending that chapter. I made my way back to the car and texted my wife to say I love you. *I love you too,* she instantly replied. I drove home and went up to the room where she was sitting watching repeats of the Friends TV show. "I've just been sacked," I said. She was so supportive and, in that moment, I knew that all those thoughts in that evening were now a thing of the past, I'd never allow anyone to ever make me feel like that ever again. I was now able to fully step into my role as The Soul Man and as a result we would grow more than I could ever imagine.

Perhaps in our pain and heartbreak, in our brokenness and our despair, WE ARE NEVER, EVER LESS THAN WHOLE, and the future is always wide open.

Jeff Foster

Chapter 16

Our community grows

How we treat people defines who we are. It drives connection or disconnection, and as I was now free to focus fully on the business, I was now able to be what I was always meant to be - the leader of our community. Everyone loved the shop, and the lease was coming to an end, and it was time to grow into something bigger and just at the perfect time but this wouldn't be without challenge. There was a shop empty up in the main street in a prime location, money was still tight so I did not know how I could move the business to something bigger when we didn't have the finances to do so. I sat in the shop in November and asked spirit "what do you guys want?" This time I sat in the comfortable hub that was once a shell and now like a warm comfortable living room. I was too comfortable and that had to change because in order to grow we must seek discomfort as I knew all too well. They responded that it was time to move forward. So, I walked up to the main street and stared into the empty shop and imagined what it would look like with us inside. I did this over and over for weeks using my imagination to powerfully create this dream. I finally made the call and agreed to a viewing. The day of the viewing came, and I stepped into the new shop, it felt instantly right. I then ran down to the shop to grab Claire, also known as Cosmic Claire! She is one of our amazing team members who had worked with me previously and was the first team member I officially employed. Claire is now our Team Manager and works alongside the team to support them in their roles. Supporting the team is vital in the development of the shop. Claire came and viewed the shop and she felt exactly the same. I said excitedly that we would take it, trusting that we would find a way to get everything sorted in 8 weeks. By this time, it was January

2020, and we had a buzzing community of people who were customers, attended classes and workshops and had all become good friends. Community is everything and it is the heart of everything that we do, it's so important to me that our community feel valued as do my team and customers. My view is that I work for my team and my customers, and the team works for the community. The power of people is nothing short of astounding in my eyes. People inspire me, they move me in many different ways, and I was about to see again the amazing power of people. When people feel valued and looked after they will do anything to help you and that's why kindness is so very important. It's not always easy to be kind, especially if someone is being particularly difficult, but with kindness you can change any situation for the better.

I had this deep ingrained feeling that we would get the new shop and we would move, and nothing was going to stop that. However, we needed a lump sum to pay our deposit and get in, and I had no idea how that was going to happen, but I just trusted that it would. I told everyone that I needed to raise as much money as I could to make this happen, and our community was fully behind us. They started talking to me and asking what they could do to raise funds, telling me that they needed the shop, it was their lifeline. At this point it would have been much easier to just stay in the old shop and renew our lease but this uncomfortable feeling pushing me out was overwhelming, we had to make this happen so our community started to give us donations in the most amazing gestures. I put the money aside and gradually over the weeks our pot started to grow! It was looking like this may actually happen, I couldn't believe it, through the power of our people the dream was becoming possible.

Society teaches us that as we grow that we need to work hard for everything we want, and although that can be true, what it strangely doesn't teach us is that it's important to accept when people want to help. I was battling with this, but people wouldn't take no for an answer as they wanted to help. I had asked the spirit world for help so if I was to refuse the help being given then what was the point in asking? Of course, the help would come from our community, and of course the spirit world would inspire them to help just the same way they had inspired me to start our business. So, if you are sitting there thinking you need help and everyone around you is offering to help, then my best advice to you, my friend, is accept that help and say thank you. I remember watching my parents argue with friends and family members who were offering help saying "no, no I'll get that, we'll make do". They were often too proud to say thank you, and this was deeply ingrained in me, so I knew I had to change my thinking on this in order to be in a vibration of acceptance. What my community was about to do next was nothing short of amazing, the kindness that people showed was about to be one of the biggest manifestations of true love and kindness.

It was a Sunday evening at the shop, and I was just about to start my Spiritual Development class. I had just run a Law of Attraction workshop with three groups of people, and I was a walking and talking example of the Law of Attraction meaning I was feeling excited, motivated, and good in my overall self. About 6:50pm the usual people started coming along to the class, then to my surprise more people came in, those who usually attended the Thursday class. What were they all doing here? Then more people started coming and before I knew it the shop was filled with people from all our classes, workshops, and customers. "Steven, you need to sit down, we have something to tell you. We have all been working hard in the background to raise the funds for the shop and we would like to give you this." They handed me a large white envelope and a card. Inside the card there were so many names and messages. Then I opened the envelope and to my shock they had filled the envelope with money. They had all been fundraising and we now had almost enough to get into the new shop! Our community had come together unprompted and wanted to help saying those familiar words I had heard before "you do so much to help other people now let us help you." At that moment, my first words were "I can't accept this" and then I started to cry, overwhelmed with emotion. "Thank you" I said as they all hugged me tight. That night when everyone went home, I sat in the shop on my own in tears not quite believing what had happened and I took to social media to thank everyone publicly for their kindness and how now there was only a small amount to raise before the dream became a reality. Then the most amazing thing happened. Someone messaged me and offered the remaining balance, she has asked me to keep her name anonymous and her gesture of help. We now had what we needed and with that message I then transferred the funds to get the new shop.

Within a week we had a contract to sign and a week later the keys for the shop. I stood there that day as the postman handed me the keys in a bubble wrapped envelope, in awe of what had just happened. Something bigger was going on, something unsettling and I couldn't explain what it was. I sat that day doing a reading for three people. They had come in for tea leaf readings and I could feel a shift in the energy of the world. I remember saying to these girls "something big is coming and it will change the whole world as we know it". Looking back, how I knew was beyond me, but I could feel a notable change in the air. Before long, this change was revealed. It was Covid-19. Since then, one of those girls has been back in very recently and reminded me of this conversation. Perhaps this is a confirmation that my psychic skills are intact! As it happened, in the second week in March, the Prime Minister announced that Covid-19 had reached British soil and that everyone was to stop non-essential travel and contact. It will be fine, everyone thought! Some weeks later whilst decorating the new shop on the evening of the 10th of May, the Prime Minister announced to STAY AT HOME. We were about to move into one of the most difficult situations right at the time we were moving shop.

A global pandemic was sweeping its way across the globe and would cast uncertainty on our business and millions of people all over the world.

When we give cheerfully and accept gratefully, everyone is blessed.

Maya Angelou

Finding the Medium Within You - 7

All the way through this book I've spoken about kindness and acceptance of self. In order to be the best medium, we can be we must also spin what I call our three wheels - the Mind, the Body, and the Soul. But what does that mean?

Take 3 circles and push them together on the edges and what you're left with is an inverted diamond shape, that diamond is you. If you aren't looking after one of these circles the diamond in the middle becomes distorted and the other two have to compensate to keep the structure.

I want you to think about it for a moment. Are you healthy in your mind, body, and your soul? You may be the greatest athlete on earth but have an unhealthy mind, so in your mental and spiritual health you will always be seeking something else. No matter how many riches you have in your life, the emotional and spiritual wellbeing is off and distorted, even though you have the house, car, and money you want. Some of the most successful people in the world are also some of the unhappiest people.

The Mind
Think of the mind as a muscle, we must feed it and protect it every day, we must give it nurture and exercise and if we let it run away with itself it will do everything it can to keep us safe. But how can we grow and experience true growth without feeling a little uncomfortable? So, the truth is that the mind must always be stretched and challenged and given rest and care just like a muscle in order for it to grow.

The Body
It goes without saying that the body must be exercised and pushed past its limits every day in order for it to grow but rest and rejuvenation is vital too, and in my experience allowing the body the

right amount of rested sleep. I wake at 5am every morning to exercise, some days it's just a walk with the dogs and others it's a run or lifting weights. The importance of this is that I get up early before I even have time for the mind to talk me out of it (the mind trying to keep me safe). Then as I run or as I walk or lift those weights, the mind recognises that this feels good, and wants more of it, and before long the mind and body talk to each other as one organism. One complete brain if you like.

The Spirit

The spirit is the strength of the mind, the part of us that connects to body and soul. The mind is our sense of psyche and intellect and should not be confused with the soul. When the mind and body are strong then the strength of the mind is invincible, the soul resonates at a high level giving us an overall feeling of wellness, much like the mind. The body needs exercise and rest, and for me that exercise is tapping into the subconscious and superconscious. What's happening here is I am meditating, I'm allowing myself to be aware of my thoughts, as nobody can clear their thoughts. I have awareness and fascination of my thoughts, and I can watch and discern what thoughts are my own and what thoughts belong to the superconscious mind - the mind of the universe, God the divine - and filtered through that superconscious mind is the knowledge of everything that was, is and will be and the thoughts of the spirit world.

So, in summary, in order for us to get to the Spirit part of mind, body and soul and reach a level of consciousness beyond our awareness, we must focus on our mental health, our physical health and spiritual health. The important thing to know is that we are always juggling the three, we are never fully developed, we are always keeping those balls in the air. Being comfortable, although it's a nice place to be temporarily, it is not a place where growth can happen and as we grow and move through stages of life our mind, body and soul, the balls will change constantly. When we stop seeking comfort we grow beyond our limits, and this is the same for mediumship. My best advice to any budding, developing mediums and anyone else who wants to be the best version of themselves, is to always seek discomfort as it's the only way you will ever grow.

Do you feel there's an area you need to work on with yourself?

- **The mind**
- **The body**
- **The spirit**

Make a detailed plan of where you want to be.

Could mediumship be something you would want to investigate?

Life is but the expression of spirit through matter. To make life manifest requires the union of spirit and body

Dr D.D. Palmer

Chapter 17
Growing

I sat in the old shop numb, all my team couldn't come to work, they had to stay at home, and I had 2 weeks to get the old shop and move everything into the new shop. How on earth was I going to manage? Strangely I had this unwavering belief secured by the spirit world that it was all going to be okay, so I stayed focussed and worked by myself on the old shop and new shop. Nobody was around so I had lots of time to work on the new shop which was a blessing in disguise. I felt completely empowered now I was in my real role as The Soul Man. I had nobody to answer to, no emails every day, it felt quiet and so peaceful. Over the next two weeks I worked the hardest I've physically worked in my adult life to get the old shop emptied and painted to hand over the keys.

My friend helped me move the furniture with his van and what looked like so much in the old shop now looked so sparse in the new shop. We had rooms to build and lots of space to fill but all this was in our fundraising budget, so we were able to get what we needed to make it all happen. The old shop was finally empty. Finally, I managed to paint it all to get it all clean and ready for its next occupant. The new shop felt a little cold and empty even with all our furniture inside, but what was missing? The soul of the shop was still in the old shop! So, I got a large box and took it to the old shop and said out loud "fill this box with your soul, everything we've created here please enter the box overnight." The next day I went back into the old shop, and it felt cold and not the same as it always had. The box was heavier now. I know this sounds strange but magically overnight the soul of the shop its essence had transferred to the box. So, I carried the box up to the new shop and opened the box and said now fill this new space, fill the walls with the same love you gave the old place and sure enough the next day walking into the new shop felt like entering the old shop. I went to the old shop and said goodbye and thanked the spirit world and the space for everything over the last two years. I locked the door and turned my key in the shutter for the last time. As the shutter came down, I stepped back so grateful and dropped the keys into the landlord's letter box which was just across the street. The next chapter was so unknown with the Covid pandemic in full swing, but I was doing the right thing, not going back now.

As the building works at the new shop carried on, every brush stroke done by myself, I had so much time to dream, and dream I did. We would teach here as well as do all the things we already did, our team will grow here much like when you put a goldfish in a larger tank that same would happen here it would inevitably grow bigger. I sat one day in May with my coffee and asked spirit once again, "what do I do here? How do I grow in a pandemic? Mediumship mentorship I heard, but how on earth can I make that happen?"

Then like magic, people were using Zoom to communicate with each other, and I could apply this to our business too, so with that I created a post on social media about a two-year mediumship mentorship programme, beginning on zoom. I knew that the first chunk of learning to be a medium is all about learning about yourself and embarking on a journey of self-discovery. Sixty-three people applied within 72 hours and a few at the last minute before the deadline. There was no way I could take on that number of students, so I had to carefully vet each application and make a decision based on my gut instincts and the guidance of the spirit world. I whittled it down to 35 people and had to say no to so many people, if you are reading this, I am sorry that it wasn't the right time for you. I had my people and now I had to email them all to tell them they were part of the course and at that moment The Soul Man Academy was officially born! People started to ask if we were doing other courses and with all my spare time, I started putting all of my skill and knowledge into writing online courses that could then be applied to in person after the pandemic. Every course I put up we had full attendance and before long I was working 4 nights a week delivering courses and teaching the LEAF Approach, kindness, and the skills it takes to be an intuitive reader! I was loving every minute of this as I was always meant to be teaching it just hasn't happened in the way I wanted. The shop at this point was getting on every day and we had lots of time to get it sorted with no real end in sight with the UK lockdown.

Tea Leaf reading, Tarot reading, Mediumship, Meditation teacher, all these training courses were helping us to reach a worldwide audience but mainly just the UK. We were building our amazing community further and further and people loved the way they felt on Zoom too. I soon realised that the feeling people get when they come to our shop comes from me and is translated through our team and then to our customers, the vibration of kindness helping us grow in ways beyond our understanding. That's the reason I have threaded through this whole book, both in the medium training sections and in the story itself, kindness is everything - it makes the world go round. It's difficult for people to be bad to someone who is kind and considerate. Kindness creates connection. It makes human interaction positive, and people feel valued and cared for, and this was translating through everything we were doing. I was so very proud of what was happening. With all of that we were creating our culture and the way people treated each other was also with the vibration of kindness.

My vision as our company grows is to empower people to be the best version of themselves physically, mentally, and spiritually. As we moved out of the pandemic, we also recruited three new team members from our training academy, people who knew how we worked and had already been working in our vibration of kindness. We had a shop that had survived in uncertain times and a business built on a dream, I needed help with the invisible side of the business and with so much new work again I asked the spirit world to help and through our mediumship mentorship we welcomed the amazing Gina, our Business Development Manager, and our wonderful Cosmic Claire, who is our Team Manager, to help me support customers and the team to the highest level. We were now operating on a new level and The Soul Man and Friends, and The Soul Man Academy, were now operating as separate entities that worked and intertwined together. People training with us would want to come into the shop as customers and people as customers wanted to train with us in a wonderful duality.

As our training Academy develops, we will strive for the best working mediums, working responsibly and from the heart. We will train people to be aware of when people need more and be able to help them by signposting and making appropriate judgement, and above all we will operate from a place of kindness and care. With grounded mediumship and psychic work, as well as truth and integrity being at the forefront of everything we do. The Soul Man and Friends was always my dream. It was always just in some other form, I feel for the first time I am truly following my path, by following the signs and letting the energy of the unseen guide me every single day. Not many people can say they work with an invisible army every day. The spirit world has helped me to create everything you see today, from being a tiny baby I was so trusting of these beings of light to through my childhood as I tried hard to ignore them, and then to being an adult and fully embracing everything they have shown me even in my most trying times they have been the one constant that never left me no matter what.

"You will be on the stage one day, Steven" my Granny used to say, "you have a warmth and love of life, and people that others will be attracted to". For me, my position allows me to help and inspire more and more people every single day. I feel loved and respected by many people, and for me being kind and helping people is so much easier than being the opposite. Those whispers as a baby in my crib perhaps they've been telling me my whole life that I will do more, I will help many. I have already helped many even as I write these words. I am acutely aware of the spirit world all around me cheering me on to the last paragraphs of the book. When we do what we are always meant to do, the universe, spirit world, and mind, body, and soul respond in wonderful and magical ways. Everything opens up and you draw the right people, places, and events into your life, it sounds so simple it's almost complicated. And because I operate from this way of thinking and being, the wonderful world of spirit responds by helping me actually train the superconscious, giving me more enriching experiences that only make me a better medium and man in a world that is oh so confusing.

I am The Soul Man. I wasn't always known as The Soul Man but over the years my ancestors, my loved ones, and the people assigned to me from my birth have gently guided me be The Soul Man and to the place I am at today. I am still developing myself, always trying to be a better version of myself so I can help my team and my family. I am so excited to see these next steps and having just navigated through a pandemic, and also finished a two-year mediumship diploma with those amazing human beings who I love so dearly, I embark upon a new journey with the next amazing bunch of new mediums. I will take my guidance from the unseen army, I will continue to be kind and grow my amazing business to new levels with determination and grit but above all with learning every single day. I thank the unseen world every single day for everything they have done to this point and to the work we will continue to do moving forwards, I work for them, and they work for me.

The medium's job is to prove the existence of the human soul beyond reasonable doubt, and to look after themselves spiritually, mentally, and physically so as they can be the best most conductive vessel, the rest is just an illusion. I can do this life, but I have to work hard every day as nothing comes by chance, only by design, and my friend there is a greater design that even I am not aware of. Every single one of us on this planet has something to give this world. You matter more than you could ever imagine.

The dragonfly is a symbol of hope and resilience that no matter what happens these insects have been around for millennia and although they haven't changed, they go through multiple changes in their short life. The dragonfly flies faster after change than it could have ever crawled in its previous incarnation. However, the dragonfly cannot communicate with the previous incarnations because it has developed into something different, something wiser and stronger than before. No matter what you are going through, no matter how difficult it may seem, you are stronger than you will ever know and what you're going through is always just temporary, even in this life.

What I have now is an unshakeable dream and a synergetic relationship with myself and my unseen army and I can't wait to leap into every uncomfortable situation life throws at me with the knowledge and power that the spirit world has my back. Unshakeable in the truth that the human soul is eternal and always evolving just like we do here on earth. Unshakeable in my belief that people are not bad, everyone has goodness in them that can be cultivated in kindness. Unshakeable in the belief that I am here to be The Soul Man, a man who is a soul doing my best to help as many people as I can through love and kindness. And unshakeable in the knowledge that the people who work closest with me will resonate on that same level.

I can't wait to see what's next, even as I write this, I know the next story is already unfolding and it's going to be exciting. Thank you for choosing me, unseen world. Thank you.

The Soul Man x

Never let fear stop you from dancing on the moon.

Join our growing community!

thesoulmanscotland.com

facebook.com/thesoulmanandfriends
instagram.com/thesoulmanandfriends
twitter.com/TheSoulManAndF1
tiktok.com/@theofficialsoulman

Scan this QR code for our website:

Come to our shop in Broxburn, West Lothian, Scotland for a reading with one of our amazing team of readers! We offer tea leaf readings, tarot readings, mediumship readings, reiki and more! Book your reading online at www.thesoulmanscotland.com/book

We also do readings over video call.

Find us at 46-48 East Main St, Broxburn, West Lothian, EH52 5AE.

Acknowledgements

I would like to acknowledge the following people who have helped me bring the dream of The Soul Man and Friends and this book to fruition. I have had to keep names and specifics out of the book as there's so many to mention.

To my lovely wife Nicola and to my beautiful children who have heard all about the book and seen the trials and tribulations of launching a new business.

To Gina for all your hard work and dedication in encouraging me and working with me to develop and edit the book to its final draft, and for continuously moving the business forward in the many areas of development. It has not been easy at times, but we turn up and continue to play the game every day.

To Claire, thank you for the hard work you've put in over the years, helping me develop new ideas and working with the team and myself. Thank you for your patience and kindness, you were there in the genesis of the Soul Man and Friends, our friendship has grown stronger and continues to do so.

To the lovely Becca for coming across from Canada to spend time with us and designing the artwork for the cover of the book, I am eternally grateful for your wonderful work that has captured the essence of my work.

To my dearest Dawn, thank you for persuading me to do this.

To the past and current Soul Man Team for all the amazing work at the shop and outwith.

To our amazing customers who have come in strangers and return time and time again as friends.

To my friend Luke for reading its final drafts and giving me encouragement.

To my beautiful little cousin Jade from Savvy VP for proofreading one of the final edits, helping to polish a rough diamond!

And thank you to you, the reader, for buying this book, I hope you find it interesting and share it with many people.

These pages here are for your notes, you can use these for the exercises given in the **Finding the Medium Within You** or just to make notes on your own experiences with spirit:

www.thesoulmanscotland.com

Printed in Great Britain
by Amazon